Collaborating with Families

A Case Study Approach

Sheri Overton

PEARSON

Merrill
Prentice Hall

Upper Saddle River, New Jersey
Columbus, Ohio

Library of Congress Cataloging-in-Publication Data

Overton, Sheri.

Collaborating with families : a case study approach / Sheri Overton.

p. cm.

ISBN 0-13-889445-0

1. Children with disabilities—Family relationships—Case studies. 2. Parents of children with disabilities—Case studies. 3. Parenting—Case studies. I. Title.

HQ773.6.O78 2005

649'.151—dc22

2004004052

Vice President and Executive Publisher: Jeffery W. Johnston
Acquisitions Editor: Allyson P. Sharp
Editorial Assistant: Kathleen S. Burk
Associate Editor: Martha Flynn
Production Editor: Linda Hillis Bayma
Text Design and Production Coordination: PreMediaONE, a Black Dot Group Company
Design Coordinator: Diane C. Lorenzo
Cover Designer: Terry Rohrbach
Cover Image: Index Stock
Production Manager: Susan Hannahs
Director of Marketing: Ann Castel Davis
Marketing Manager: Autumn Purdy
Marketing Coordinator: Tyra Poole

This book was set in Times by PreMediaONE, a Black Dot Group Company.
The cover was printed by Phoenix Color Corp.

Pearson Prentice Hall™ is a trademark of Pearson Education, Inc.
Pearson® is a registered trademark of Pearson plc
Prentice Hall® is a registered trademark of Pearson Education, Inc.
Merrill® is a registered trademark of Pearson Education, Inc.

Pearson Education Ltd.
Pearson Education Singapore Pte. Ltd.
Pearson Education Canada, Ltd.
Pearson Education—Japan

Pearson Education Australia Pty. Limited
Pearson Education North Asia Ltd.
Pearson Educación de Mexico, S.A. de C.V.
Pearson Education Malaysia Pte. Ltd.

10 9 8 7 6 5 4 3 2
ISBN: 0-13-889445-0

Preface

The idea for this book must have germinated for years before it suddenly popped up in a moment of insight. As a teacher–educator and parent, I always tried to share my respect for families with the students in my classes. I told stories about the many families I knew and invited numerous parents to speak to my classes. Although students were typically inspired and gained valuable insights, they were not fully aware of the wide range of parents they would meet in their classrooms. I wanted to facilitate my students' understanding and respect for the variety of families with which they would work.

I began to ask family members to write their stories for me. I sought to obtain a good mixture of people from across the country, from different income levels and personal histories, from diverse racial and ethnic groups, who had children with various disabilities at various ages. I drew on a number of individuals I met from living and working in various parts of the country. In addition, I contacted other individuals around the country to ask if they were aware of individuals who would be willing to share their stories. These contacts included teachers and administrators, parent e-mail groups, parent centers, and others whom I knew had some interaction with individuals with disabilities. I particularly wanted to include individuals whom others would not consider active in their children's schools or disability organizations, and I looked for fathers and others whom educators may not know as well. The family members wrote or dictated their stories with minimal direction from me. As time passed, I asked for elaboration or clarification of their stories. While I provided some editing or rearranging to make the cases more useable, I was committed to making minimal changes to preserve the tone of each storyteller's voice. I felt that it was important that the individuals be heard and respected just as they were in reality, rather than polished versions. To check the suitability of the story resulting from my editing, family members read and approved my versions. All names were changed to preserve confidentiality.

The activities, margin notes, and commentaries developed over time to emphasize and clarify points, facilitate reflection, tie theory and research to the story, and occasionally to correct the misinformation presented by parents. Even though parents do not always operate with the most accurate or current information, the publisher and I were committed to publishing accurate information for teacher preparation. All of the cases have been field tested and reviewed multiple times, allowing revision to enhance their use. The result is a set of diverse cases that have been successful in stimulating reflection and discussion and, I hope, more reflective practice. It is my hope that, at the end of your work with this book, you will have developed many resources and ideas for working with families. To that end, each case asks you to determine and discuss the best practices that would support and facilitate collaboration with each family.

ACKNOWLEDGMENTS

Support for this effort has come in many forms and from many individuals. Foremost, this book would not have been possible without the commitment and openness of the family members who wrote these cases. Their willingness to reveal their lives to others was based on a desire to help others understand families and to improve professional practice. Several of the family members confided that telling their stories was simultaneously a gut-wrenching and therapeutic experience. For their efforts, I will be eternally grateful. I am also appreciative to the many individuals who worked to help me locate families.

Cecilia Silva of Texas Christian University provided the translation for Maria's case, both working alone and spending hours in meetings with Maria and me. Her warmth and compassion, together with her knowledge of the field and cultural and linguistic intricacies, made possible this important contribution to the book. I want to thank Doug and Rich Simpson, who served as mentors in the initial stages of developing a prospectus and finding a publisher. Other friends have encouraged me and helped me to sustain momentum because they believed in the importance of this book. In some cases, these friends also provided help by reading and commenting on sections or by using the cases in classes and sharing comments from students. Special thanks go to Sue Anderson, Linda Hanson, Neil Houser, Sharon Maroney, Nancy Meadows, Diana Moore, Denise Mundorf, Mary Patton, and Mary Ann Black.

I would also like to acknowledge the following individuals who reviewed the manuscript and made suggestions for improvements: Kelly M. Anderson, University of North Carolina at Charlotte; James F. Austin, University of Akron; Greg Conderman, St. Ambrose University; Louise Fulton, California State University at San Bernadino; Linda Schwartz Green, Centenary College; James E. Hollis, Walla Walla College; Linda M. Mitchell, Witchita State University; Mary O'Brian, Illinois State University; Robert Ortiz, California State University at Fullerton; E. Michelle Pardew, Western Oregon University; Alec Peck, Boston College; Rose Marie Pryor, University of Cincinnati; and Ellen Williams, Bowling Green State University. At Merrill/Prentice Hall, I had the good fortune to work with Ann Davis and Allyson Sharp. They were extremely patient and made important suggestions that helped me produce a much better book.

Lastly, I wish to express my love and appreciation to my mother, my sister and brother-in-law, and Steve, who have been especially solid supports this past year, and to my daughter Kate, her fiancé Kenny, and my son Aaron, who have been sources of great pride and inspiration. They continue to teach me what it means to be a family.

Discover the Companion Website
Accompanying This Book

THE PRENTICE HALL COMPANION WEBSITE:
A VIRTUAL LEARNING ENVIRONMENT

Technology is a constantly growing and changing aspect of our field that is creating a need for content and resources. To address this emerging need, Prentice Hall has developed an online learning environment for students and professors alike—Companion Websites—to support our textbooks.

In creating a Companion Website, our goal is to build on and enhance what the textbook already offers. For this reason, the content for each user-friendly website is organized by topic and provides the professor and student with a variety of meaningful resources. Common features of a Companion Website include:

For the Professor—

Every Companion Website integrates **Syllabus Manager**™, an online syllabus creation and management utility.

- **Syllabus Manager**™ provides you, the instructor, with an easy, step-by-step process to create and revise syllabi, with direct links into the Companion Website and other online content without having to learn HTML.

- Students may logon to your syllabus during any study session. All they need to know is the web address for the Companion Website and the password you've assigned to your syllabus.

- After you have created a syllabus using **Syllabus Manager**™, students may enter the syllabus for their course section from any point in the Companion Website.

- Clicking on a date, the student is shown the list of activities for the assignment. The activities for each assignment are linked directly to actual content, saving time for students.

- Adding assignments consists of clicking on the desired due date, then filling in the details of the assignment—name of the assignment, instructions, and whether it is a one-time or repeating assignment.

- In addition, links to other activities can be created easily. If the activity is online, a URL can be entered in the space provided, and it will be linked automatically in the final syllabus.

- Your completed syllabus is hosted on our servers, allowing convenient updates from any computer on the Internet. Changes you make to your syllabus are immediately available to your students at their next logon.

For the Student—

- **Overview and General Information** – General information about the topic and how it will be covered in the website.

- **Web Links** – A variety of websites related to topic areas.

- **Content Methods and Strategies** – Resources that help to put theories into practice in the special education classroom.

- **Reflective Questions and Case-Based Activities** – Put concepts into action, participate in activities, examine strategies, and more.

- **National and State Laws** – An online guide to how federal and state laws affect your special education classroom.

- **Behavior Management** – An online guide to help you manage behaviors in the special education classroom.

- **Message Board**—Virtual bulletin board to post and respond to questions and comments from a national audience.

To take advantage of these and other resources, please visit the *Collaborating with Families: A Case Study Approach* Companion Website at

www.prenhall.com/overton

EDUCATOR LEARNING CENTER: AN INVALUABLE ONLINE RESOURCE

Merrill Education and the Association for Supervision and Curriculum Development (ASCD) invite you to take advantage of a new online resource, one that provides access to the top research and proven strategies associated with ASCD and Merrill— the Educator Learning Center. At **www.EducatorLearningCenter.com** you will find resources that will enhance your students' understanding of course topics and of current

educational issues, in addition to being invaluable for further research.

How the Educator Learning Center will Help Your Students Become Better Teachers

With the combined resources of Merrill Education and ASCD, you and your students will find a wealth of tools and materials to better prepare them for the classroom.

Research

- More than 600 articles from the ASCD journal *Educational Leadership* discuss everyday issues faced by practicing teachers.
- A direct link on the site to Research Navigator™ gives students access to many of the leading education journals, as well as extensive content detailing the research process.
- Excerpts from Merrill Education texts give your students insights on important topics of instructional methods, diverse populations, assessment, classroom management, technology, and refining classroom practice.

Classroom Practice

- Hundreds of lesson plans and teaching strategies are categorized by content area and age range.
- Case studies and classroom video footage provide virtual field experience for student reflection.
- Computer simulations and other electronic tools keep your students abreast of today's classrooms and current technologies.

Look into the Value of Educator Learning Center Yourself

A four-month subscription to Educator Learning Center is $25 but is **FREE** when used in conjunction with this text. To obtain free passcodes for your students, simply contact your local Merrill/Prentice Hall sales representative, and your representative will give you a special ISBN to give your bookstore when ordering your textbooks. To preview the value of this website to you and your students, please go to **www.EducatorLearningCenter.com** and click on "Demo."

Brief Contents

Contents

Part One

Stories and Today's Society

CHAPTER ONE

Stories as Tools for Learning

S napshots make life look simple, but real life is complicated. A deeper look into any family's life will reveal whatever you look for—stories of love, adventure, mystery, or great courage; tales of overcoming great odds; as well as comedy, irony, heart-rending sorrow, disappointment, loss, or missed opportunities. As professionals, we seldom know enough of these stories to realize all that occurs in particular family situations. We are not there to witness a young boy as he squeals with laughter and watches in adoration as his uncle puts together a tricycle. It would require an intimate knowledge of a family to know that a wife and husband lie awake at night and discuss how to pay for after-school child care. The teacher is unaware that a mother at the laundromat is showing her 9-year-old child how to measure a cup of soap into the washer. These and countless other hidden snapshots depict how families contribute to their children's development in complex ways.

THE STORY OF THESE STORIES

About the Families

This book presents the real-life stories of families who have children with special needs. These families are at the same time ordinary and extraordinary. They come from various rural, urban, and suburban communities across the United States. They have children of various ages, as well as different incomes, different lifestyles, and a range of experiences with educational systems, which are sometimes satisfactory and beneficial and sometimes problematic. Some of the families have frequent and substantive interactions with their children's teachers and some are relatively unknown to the educators involved. The families have children with a range of disabilities. The stories are as varied as the families involved; however, their children, their family configurations, and their approaches to rearing and educating their children will sound familiar to many teachers.

The family members' candor and the richness of their storytelling expose extraordinary qualities. One is struck by fierce protectiveness, extraordinary perseverance, touching tenderness, uncommon resourcefulness, warrior spirit, skilled diplomacy, quick humor, and love that transcends explanation. In recognizing their strengths, it may be tempting to assume that these families are stronger or are more committed than the families with which one typically comes into contact and to miss the point that all families have strengths. These are not all known to their schools as families with involved parents, and if approached from a deficit model, a very different picture of each family could emerge. These are the families of students with whom teachers are working all over the country, with their strengths and their flaws.

The family members tell the stories themselves, which convey the passions and concerns of the individuals in moving and thought-provoking ways. The stories were produced in various mediums: some on handwritten pages of notebook paper, some on e-mail, one on tape recordings, and some on typed and edited pages. In one case, the family member wrote the story in Spanish, a third party translated the story, and finally the story was checked through a three-way meeting. Although each case may have been reorganized and edited to facilitate your understanding, the family member's voice, their manner of expression, and their interpretation of personal experiences are maintained in an authentic manner so that you gain an appreciation and respect for the thoughts and feelings of individuals with diverse communicative styles and varying degrees of expressive ability. You should acknowledge the diversity of the voices, reflect on your own intellectual and emotional responses to the family member's style of communication, and be open to the message that the family member is trying to convey. These are not professional writers; however, their stories carry the richness of real people.

Reading the thoughts of "real people" may challenge you in ways that a traditional text will not. Personal communications can contain ambiguities, unanswered questions, and facts that may be erroneous. Rather than ease this challenge for you, it is hoped that you will gain from it. If you find yourself confused, offended, angered, or impatient with someone's words, you have an opportunity to thoughtfully consider how you would respond to a similar face-to-face communication. In the context of this book and the related coursework, you can reflect on and discuss with classmates your perceptions of the family members' communication styles, their personalities, and the probable effects on your efforts to collaborate with them.

The Book's Objectives

This book was written to assist teachers and other helping professionals in the development of a respectful and insightful collaborative approach to working with families. The book's premise is that such an approach is best facilitated by viewing life, and especially schools, through the eyes of the family members of children with special needs. From a case approach, teachers have an opportunity to listen to a parent's thinking, to hear how a perspective has developed through various experiences, and to identify with a parent's needs. When you "step inside" the family's perspective, you can identify strategies to support the family, forge a stronger relationship with the family members, and ultimately maximize your students' learning. You will hear only the family member's voice and perspective in these stories, which is the perspective that is less familiar to educators; however, you are encouraged to acknowledge and discuss alternative perspectives as well.

These stories serve as a rich context to examine, discuss, and practice the concepts and skills presented in coursework for educators and the other professionals related to parent or family collaboration. The book is intended to supplement a traditional textbook by providing readings and activities that may be aligned with typical course content. In addition to reinforcing and expanding course content, the following objectives were established:

- You will gain a better appreciation for the complexity of families and recognize that relying on stereotypes and assumptions is inadequate.

- Your approach to families will be characterized by first looking for and then building upon their strengths and the manner in which the families support their children, rather than on highlighting their deficits.

- You will refrain from oversimplifying a family's or an individual's problem as an indication that they do not care about their children.

- You will gain a better understanding of the stresses and demands of families who have members with special needs and how those stresses and demands can impact their relationship with you.

- You will be aware of the barriers as perceived by families that systems or individual professionals devise to the attainment of appropriate services and how those barriers can affect families.

- You will be aware of teachers' attitudes and behaviors that empower families and make family members want to collaborate with teachers and the attitudes and behaviors that make family members feel frustrated, angry, or disinterested.

A RATIONALE FOR CASE STUDY

There are many forms of delivery used in college coursework, including lecture, group discussion, and case study. The case study method offers several unique advantages. This method uses the narrative accounts of real individuals, with "enough intriguing decision points and provocative undercurrents to make a discussion group want to think and argue about them" (Hansen, 1987, p. 265). The use of real cases causes you to tie theory to practice, and the stories function as a substitute for direct experiences that may be missing (Jonassen & Hernandez-Serrano, 2002). As the concepts reappear in different cases, a more complex understanding evolves, as well as the ability to recognize the concepts in new situations (Barnett & Ramirez, 1996). By identifying the relevance of old situations to new situations, you can decide when previously used strategies should be repeated or when they should be avoided (Kolodner, 1997).

Case study also fosters critical analysis and reflection (Hyun & Marshall, 1997; McNaughton, Hall, & Maccini, 2001; Paul et al., 1995; J. H. Shulman, 1996; L. S. Shulman, 1996; Silverman & Welty, 1996; Wood & Anderson, 2001; Wright, 1996). To understand how a particular case relates to theory, you must examine what you have learned from textbooks, as well as the experiences and feelings of the stories' "characters." This examination enables the development of an increased sensitivity and awareness of diverse perspectives, including sensitivity for cultural diversity (J. H. Shulman, 1996). The stories may compel you to examine issues of race, class, religion, and gender. As you connect the narratives to your life experience, you are encouraged to reflect on your own beliefs and biases.

According to constructivist learning theories, this type of critical analysis and reflection results in effective, substantive, and enduring learning (L. S. Shulman, 1996; Williams, 1996). You are actively engaged in case analysis and discussion, and you take on a greater responsibility for learning than in the traditionally passive role of a lecture format. By working on problems in context, you learn to approach new situations in this same active, analytic, problem-solving manner. There is an emphasis on multiple perspectives, which not only causes you to question your assumptions, but it also causes you to question how you reached those assumptions. In addition, case use helps to uncover personal biases and the influences of past experiences. You work in dialogue with others, in an environment where you and your fellow students feel safe to voice your differing views. (L. S. Shulman, 1996; Williams, 1996).

THE CASE STUDY PROCESS

Course Design Issues

There are many ways to use cases. Case discussions may encompass only one class session or multiple sessions, with case issues often referenced again with building complexity relative to new cases. Students become more collaborative and self-directed problem solvers over time; therefore, case use over multiple courses has been advised (C. S. Barnett, 1999; Tomey, 2003). Most typically, case study is not used as the sole method of instruction. Many instructors prefer to present content in a more traditional format, using cases interspersed throughout the semester or intensely during the later part of the course (Greenwood, 1996).

Your instructor may rely on case study exclusively for class presentations. Silverman and Welty (1996) proposed moving to a discussion-based class format and abandoning lectures and overhead transparencies altogether. They believe that lecturing students for half the class, followed by discussion, caused students to expect the professor to provide the correct answers. Instead, Silverman and Welty chose a textbook that would convey the content; they discussed this content at the beginning of class through group discussion; and then they progressed to the discussion of a case that demonstrated the application of the topic. It is difficult to present lectures first and then try to engage students in active learning. Students unaccustomed to assuming an active role in learning may have more difficulty making this shift.

Another decision that course designers make is whether to use cases with whole-class discussion or to use smaller groups followed by a whole-group summary. There are advantages to both uses. Small groups provide more opportunities to speak and may draw out quiet students; however, with larger groups, the instructor's time is not divided and it is possible to observe and facilitate more of the discussion. Anderson and Baker (1999) describe how one program designed a curriculum that incorporated both large- and small-group discussions combined with interspersed journaling assignments.

Preparing for Case Discussions

Reading and thinking about the case before discussion is important, or learning will be very superficial. The important part of preparatory work is coming to class with "reasoned insights and suggestions" (Williams, 1996, p. 192). According to Silverman and Welty (1996), a typical type of preparatory assignment requires writing an analysis, using the theories you are studying to explain what is happening in the case. Your analysis demonstrates reflection on the ways in which your own experiences influence your interpretations, and

rich and abundant. Case study ties theory to practice and fosters critical analysis and reflection. The process demands that you prepare carefully for case discussions, keep an open mind and consider divergent views, support your peers in the expression of their views, think critically, and assume responsibility for your own learning. Through the study of these families' cases and the linking of their real-world perceptions to educational theory and research, educators can learn how to communicate and collaborate with them in a manner that benefits children, families, and schools.

Suggested Resources

Colbert, J. A., Desberg, P., & Trimble, K. (Eds.). (1996). *The case for education: Contemporary approaches for using case methods.* Boston: Allyn & Bacon.

Elksnin, L. K. (2001). Implementing the case method of instruction in special education teacher preparation programs. *Teacher Education and Special Education, 24*(2), 95–107.

References

Anderson, P. L., & Baker, B. K. (1999). A case-based curriculum approach to special education teacher preparation. *Teacher Education and Special Education, 22*(3), 188–192.

Barnett, C. & Ramirez, A. (1996). Fostering critical analysis and reflection through mathematics case discussion. In J. A. Colbert, P. Desberg, & K. Trimble (Eds.), *The case for education: Contemporary approaches for using case methods* (pp. 1–13). Boston: Allyn & Bacon.

Barnett, C. S. (1999). Cases. *Journal of Staff Development, 20*(3), 26–27.

Benham, M. K. P. (1996). The practitioner–scholars' view of school change: A case-based approach to teaching and learning. *Teaching & Teacher Education, 12*(2), 119–135.

Colbert, J. A. (1996). Cases in context. In J. A. Colbert, P. Desberg, & K. Trimble (Eds.), *The case for education: Contemporary approaches for using case methods* (pp. 29–37). Boston: Allyn & Bacon.

Danforth, S., & Boyle, J. R. (2000). *Cases in behavior management.* Upper Saddle River, NJ: Merrill/Prentice Hall.

Elksnin, L. K. (2001). Implementing the case method of instruction in special education teacher preparation programs. *Teacher Education and Special Education, 24*(2), 95–107.

Fey, M. H., & Sinith, C. F. (1999). Opening spaces for collaboration and inquiry in teacher education classrooms: The place of resistance. *Action in Teacher Education, 21*(3), 102–110.

Greenwood, G. E. (1996). Using the case method to translate theory into practice. In J. A. Colbert, P. Desberg, & K. Trimble (Eds.), *The case for education: Contemporary approaches for using case methods* (pp. 57–78). Boston: Allyn & Bacon.

Grupe, F. H., & Jay, J. K. (2000). Incremental cases: Real-life, real-time problem solving. *College Teaching, 48*(4), 123–128.

Hansen, A. J. (1987). Reflections of a casewriter: Writing teaching cases. In C. R. Christensen (Ed.), *Teaching and the case method* (pp. 264–270). Boston: Harvard Business School.

Hyun, E., & Marshall, J. D. (1997). Theory of multiple/multiethnic perspective-taking ability for teachers' developmentally and culturally appropriate practice (DCAP). *Journal of Research in Childhood Education, 11(*2), 188–198.

Jonassen, D. H., & Hernandez-Serrano, J. (2002). Case-based reasoning and instructional design: Using stories to support problem solving. *Educational Technology Research and Development, 50*(2), 65–77.

Kolodner, J. L. (1997). Educational implications of analogy: A view from case-based reasoning. *American Psychologist, 52*(1), 57–66.

McNaughton, D., Hall, T. E., & Maccini, P. (2001). Case-based instruction in special education teacher preparation: Practices and concerns of teacher educator/researchers. *Teacher Education and Special Education, 24*(2), 84–94.

Paul, J. L., Epanchin, B., Rosselli, H., Townsend, B. L., Cranston-Gingras, A., & Thomas, D. (1995). Addressing the inevitable conflicts in reforming teacher education: One department's story. *Journal of Learning Disabilities, 28*(10), 646–655.

Shulman, J. H. (1996). Tender feelings, hidden thoughts: Confronting bias, innocence, and racism through case discussions. In J. A. Colbert, P. Desberg, & K. Trimble (Eds.), *The case for education: Contemporary approaches for using case methods* (pp. 137–158). Boston: Allyn & Bacon.

Shulman, L. S. (1996). Just in case: Reflections on learning from experience. In J. A. Colbert, P. Desberg, & K. Trimble (Eds.), *The case for education: Contemporary approaches for using case methods* (pp. 197–217). Boston: Allyn & Bacon.

Silverman, R., & Welty, W. M. (1996). Teaching without a net: Using cases in teacher education. In J. A. Colbert, P. Desberg, & K. Trimble (Eds.), *The case for education: Contemporary approaches for using case methods* (pp. 159–171). Boston: Allyn & Bacon.

Sudzina, M. R., & Kibane, C. R. (1994, June). *New contexts for educational case study applications: From classroom to competition and beyond.* Paper presented at the annual meeting of the World Association for Case Method Research & Application, Montreal, Canada.

Tomey, A. M. (2003). Learning with cases. *Journal of Continuing Education in Nursing, 34*(1), 34–38.

Williams, M. M. (1996). Using the case method in a foundations of education course. In J. A. Colbert, P. Desberg, & K. Trimble (Eds.), *The case for education: Contemporary approaches for using case methods* (pp. 187–195). Boston: Allyn & Bacon.

Wood, A. T., & Anderson, C. H. (2001, June). *The case study method: Critical thinking enhanced by effective teacher questioning skills.* Paper presented at the 2001 Annual International Conference of the World Association for Case Method Research & Application. (ERIC Document Reproduction Service No. ED455221)

Wright, S. (1996). Case-based instruction: Linking theory to practice. *Physical Educator, 53*(4), 190–197.

Two or more people who regard themselves as a family and who perform some of the functions that families typically perform. These people may or may not be related by blood or marriage and may or may not usually live together. (pp. 24-25)

This definition reflects the fact that families in America have varied compositions. Even when considering only families with children, the different compositions are apparent; the children may live with one or more parents or no parents, they may have family members residing in several households, and they may live in families that include members who are not blood relatives. One or more biological parents, stepparents, adoptive parents, siblings, grandparents, same-sex parents, foster parents, or friends or romantic partners of the child's parent may head a family. Some family units include a large extended family of grandparents, aunts and uncles, and cousins. A child may live with a parent and yet have a majority of the parental functions performed by another individual, such as a child who lives with his mother but receives daily guidance and care from a grandparent or aunt. A group of siblings may be a family unit while spread out in various foster placements. A household of two or more families may live together and function as one family.

An individual's definition of family may be influenced by numerous factors, such as culture and tradition, race, sexual orientation, and economic considerations. Consider that

- According to 2000 U.S. census figures, 6.1% of the population lives in households where none of the members are related by blood or marriage. (U.S. Census Bureau, 2001).

- Many children live in one of three main types of multigenerational families residing in the same household: (a) the householder with his or her child and grandchild (2.6 million households), (b) the householder with his or her child and parent or parent in-law (1.3 million households), and (c) the householder with his or her child and grandchildren and parent or parent in-law (78,000 households; U.S. Census Bureau, 2001).

- Gay male couples and lesbian couples increasingly are choosing to have biological or adopted children. An estimated 6 million to 14 million children live with at least one gay male or lesbian parent. Legal discrimination, social discrimination, and overt hostility are still factors in the lives of gay male couples and lesbian couples; therefore, families may not be open about the family constellation. Approximately 21 states grant second-parent adoptions; therefore, the child's second mother or second father is afforded full rights in decision making (American Civil Liberties Union, 1999; Savin-Williams & Esterberg, 2000).

- African American children are three times as likely as other children to live with relatives, apart from their parents (Glick, 1997). A number of scholars have argued that slavery's chaotic effect on African American families resulted in greater variability and adaptability in family structure, including enlarged kinship networks, shared households with nonrelatives, and informal adoption of children. Other scholars have linked these extended households to the extended family traditions of West African cultures or on economic marginality that encourages the sharing of resources and emotional support (Rivers & Scanzoni, 1997; Taylor, 2000).

- Some families consist of members residing in two different countries. This may be on a temporary or somewhat permanent basis. The U.S. Immigration Service has a program to assist families in reuniting, and many immigrants, particularly Latino or Asian individuals, have come to the United States because of family sponsored migration. Although they might not live in the same household, immigrants often assemble an extended family, particularly if a sibling or other relative has acted as a sponsor during the immigration process (Zinn & Wells, 2000).

- Joint physical custody, where the child lives with both parents on a schedule of at least a 30/70 time share between parents, is an increasing option in divorce arrangements. Almost unheard of before 1970, joint custody was awarded in more than one out of five divorces in 1994 (American Divorce Network, 2003).

The Significance of Different Realities

Historian Stephanie Coontz, in *The Way We Never Were: American Families and the Nostalgia Trap* (1992) and *The Way We Really Are: Coming to Terms With America's Changing Families* (1997*)*, places American families in a historical context and demonstrates how greatly diverse families are and always have been. While there have been transformations in American family life, frequently these resulted in gains for one type of family and losses for another type of family, or what a family gained in one context was experienced as a loss in another context. According to Coontz (1992) "we must reject attempts to 'recapture' family traditions that either never existed or existed in a totally different context" (p. 5). Coontz shows that the myths of a "golden age" of families are nostalgic false generalizations. For example, divorce rates may be higher than in the 1950s; however, such statistics ignore the many legally married couples who lived apart from each other and those who stuck it out in misery. Absent parents, family violence, and children suffering in poverty were a part of the full reality of family life in past decades.

Coontz (1992) advances the idea that periods of family crisis and readjustment have always followed major changes in socioeconomic structure. Overlooking the external influences that have shaped families, and instead overemphasizing personal responsibility for strengthening family values encourages moralizing rather than building responsible social policy. Coontz's point is reiterated by scholars of African American families who argue that long-standing criticisms of the disintegration of African American families typically focus on issues of morality rather than on the economic conditions that have resulted in such changes (Sudarkasa, 1997).

What is your own concept of family? The form of your family and your family experiences influence the way you conceptualize the term, as well as what you expect from the families of your students. Because teachers work with children that come from so varied family experiences, they must be particularly reflective of their own perspectives and how they arrived at those perspectives. In addition, teachers should be aware of the limitations of their own experiences. For example, they may not have experienced racial discrimination or having a family member with a disability. This type of personal reflection helps to guard against judgmental behaviors when families look or act different, and it helps to guard against expectations that are consistent with our own lives rather than the lives of the students' families. For example, personal experience might lead a teacher to expect educational decisions from a child's mother when, in fact, it is the child's grandmother or uncle who makes the decisions in the educational arena. Building on this personal reflection, teachers can begin to learn about the families of their students and the ways in which the family members can be and want to be involved in their children's education.

THE IMPORTANCE OF FAMILIES

Families play a vital role in the education of their children. Foremost, they are generally the child's first and most invested teachers. Additionally, they create conditions that support and maximize the child's behavior and achievement at school. Families' involvement takes many forms.

Respecting What Families Do

The job of parenting a child is awesome. Parents and others who assume this role feed, bathe, clothe, and clean up after the child until the child can do these tasks independently. They model speech for the child, encourage walking and general physical development, and ensure the child's safety and well-being. They may serve as case managers for their children with disabilities, obtaining and coordinating medical services, educational services, and therapies. Families are responsible for much of what a child learns in the first years. The family typically teaches the child's first vocabulary and fosters concept development, including color and number concepts and labels. They teach the child to button and unbutton, to zip and unzip; to use eating utensils; to use the toilet; to turn on the television and use the telephone; to open a book, and to ride a tricycle. As the child grows, it is the family members who are likely to teach the child to safely negotiate the neighborhood, to care for personal belongings, to compare prices and make purchases at the store, to prepare meals, to use transportation systems, and to arrive home on time.

Another primary role of the family is to provide for the child's emotional well-being. The family provides the child with a sense of self-esteem and contributes to the child's feeling of security, it teaches the child to care for others and teaches self-discipline and responsibility, it provides values that instruct the child about right and wrong and about morality, and it serves to encourage and console the child throughout life. Not all families have the same support or resources for parenting, approach parenting in the same way or with the same passion, or achieve the same results; however, their teachings serve as the foundation for what the child will learn in school and the rest of his life.

The family is a complex system made up of its individual members, and what impacts any one of these members impacts the entire system. This perspective, called a *family systems perspective,* holds that providing for children's education is merely one of the important roles that families play. In addition to ensuring the education of family members, Turnbull and Turnbull (2001) explain that other family roles are to

- share affection and unconditional love
- foster members' self-esteem

- transmit cultural and personal spiritual beliefs

- provide for economic needs

- attend to the day-to-day needs for cooking, cleaning, hygiene, health care, transportation, and so forth

- meet members needs for socialization

- spend leisure time together and provide for family members' recreational needs

Family members must balance their activities to fulfill these eight roles and, in any family, a satisfactory balance can be difficult to achieve. Various values, aspirations, traditions, societal and cultural influences, economic conditions, or unique family characteristics will cause a family to emphasize one role over another and to arrange its priorities differently from another given family. At times, some of these roles will also temporarily shift priority because of opportunities or pressing demands, and roles will shift in priority over time as the family grows and changes. Outsiders will never fully know the forces that have influenced a family to spend more or less time on educational matters or to know what trade-offs have been made to arrive at a balance that is perceived as necessary, if not optimal.

How Families Are Involved in Education

A family's commitment of time and emotional and economic resources to educational concerns depends on many factors. To some extent, educational systems and their views of parental roles have influenced the roles families have played in their children's education. Turnbull and Turnbull (2001) note that, from a historical context, educational systems have not always considered parental involvement desirable. With training in pedagogy, the shared view was that teachers were the experts and, therefore, they knew what was best for their students. It was thought that parents possessed insufficient information to make important educational decisions; therefore, the expectation was that teachers, as experts, make recommendations and teach parents about their child's needs and how to be better parents. At times, professionals considered parents more problematic than helpful. They perceived parents as transmitting undesirable traits and characteristics that teachers should help children overcome.

These views evolved, and as concern for individual rights grew in the last half of the 20th century, so did advocacy and legislation for parent's rights in school matters. Particularly noteworthy was the passage of the Education for All Handicapped Children Act (PL 94-142) in 1975, now renamed the Individuals With Disabilities Education Act. This law gave families a legal voice in the educational decisions for their children with disabilities, and it assured due process of law to enable families to be more involved. In a subsequent reauthorization of this law, early-childhood educational planning teams were required to consider additional family needs that would affect the educational success of a child with disabilities. Other federal programs, including Title 1 of the Elementary and Secondary Education Act and Goals 2000, required that parents be included in state and local educational planning (Ballen & Moles, 1994). Over the years, families' roles in decision making, service development, service delivery, and advocacy have grown, creating more opportunities and greater expectations for parental involvement in the education of their children.

Families do not all respond to these opportunities and expectations the same, however. Some families may be comfortable relying on a teacher's expertise to make educational decisions, while some families will want to be intricately involved in many decisions. Other families are much more involved in taking care of other aspects of their family life and they may have little energy left for educational concerns. Gore and Gore (2002) have concluded that, with the struggle to make ends meet and to juggle work and family, "the quality of family life is suffering because so many working parents are now chronically exhausted, stretched thin, and stressed out" (p. 324). Many additional factors have inhibited parental involvement in their children's education, including school practices that do not accommodate families' needs, parents' past negative experiences with schools, child care and transportation needs, cultural and language differences, a sense of low self-worth on the part of impoverished parents, teachers' attitudes, and parents' uncertainty about how to be involved (White-Clark & Decker, 1996).

Family involvement also varies in typology. Many parents and other family members are active at school and are visible to educators. Data from the 1996 National Household Education Survey (as cited in Nord & West, 2001) showed that, in the general school population, 58% of mothers and 28% of fathers of students who live with two biological parents participated in at least three of the following: (a) a general school meeting; (b) a regularly scheduled parent–teacher conference; (c) a school event or class event; or (d) volunteering at school. In the Survey on Family and School Partnerships in Public Schools, K-8 (as cited in Carey, Lewis, & Farris, 1998), a national sample of elementary school principals reported that parents were more likely to attend school activities that featured some interaction with their children's teachers. Approximately half of these principals said that "most or all" parents attended parent–teacher conferences and school open houses or back-to-school nights. However, satisfaction with the degree of parental involvement decreased as the minority enrollment or poverty concentration increased. According to the U.S. Department of Education (2001), nearly 90% of the families of students with disabilities reported attending their child's IEP meeting the previous year, and more than 85% of the families attended a school meeting or conference other than an IEP. Approximately 75% of these children had an adult family member attend a school activity, and close to half of the families volunteered to help with a school activity. More than 25% of the families had attended a parent support or training workshop in the past.

Some families are more involved in education at home, perhaps in ways that are not apparent to educators. Scott-Jones (1995) noted three important ways that parents do this: (a) conveying the value of education to their children, (b) monitoring their children's behavior and performance, and (c) helping their children with the acquisition of academic skills. For example, Epstein and Lee (1995) found that most parents of eighth graders reported that they have rules about homework, chores, and maintaining grades; they place limits on watching television; and they talk regularly with their children about school. The U.S. Department of Education (2001) noted that support at home for children with disabilities appears to be very high, with 90% of parents reporting that they regularly talk to their children about school. These parents also reported that 83% help with homework three or more times a week, and 66% read to their child three or more times a week.

Families may be involved in other ways as well. Joyce Epstein (1995) described six types of partnerships that educational systems may develop with families. The first type of partnership involves assisting families with basic parenting skills, such as managing behavior, teaching responsibility and honesty, and setting up predictable schedules for the child. A second possible partnership includes communicating clearly about school programs and children's progress in school. A third partnership possibility is to involve families as volunteers in school activities to support the school and students. In the fourth type of partnership, teachers may involve families with their children in learning activities at home, including homework and projects that link curriculum to activities in the home. The fifth type of partnership possibility includes families in decision making, in school governance, in developing plans for their children, or in advocacy for policy decisions. The last type of partnership that Epstein describes is collaborating with the community to strengthen school programs, coordinating businesses, agencies, colleges, or others in the community. A comprehensive program offers families opportunities to collaborate in numerous ways across any of these categories.

In moving toward a more collaborative relationship with families, it is important to assess the opportunities we, as teachers, create for families and the behaviors that we employ to communicate those opportunities. The way in which teachers view families may influence the effectiveness of their collaborative relationships. When teachers treat families as powerful and capable advocates of the child's best interests with effective and appreciated contributions, families will be more likely to pursue this role further. If families are perceived instead as problematic, this may create guilt, resentment, or defensiveness within the families. If they are viewed as recipients of professionals' decisions rather than educational decision makers, family members may feel less encouragement to learn about the options proposed and less invested in decisions. They may also attribute more blame, as they were not involved in the decisions. It may not be at first apparent who has input into educational decisions, or who is the best family member to contact about such topics as the environment in which the child completes homework or what might be bothering the child. We, as teachers, can influence a family member's desire and ability to be involved in the educational process.

The Value of Family Involvement in Education

We know that children do better in school when their families are involved. In a publication for the U.S. Department of Education, Funkhouser and Gonzales (1997) summarized this fact:

> When families are involved in their children's education, children earn higher grades and receive higher scores on tests, attend school more regularly, complete more homework, demonstrate more positive attitudes and behaviors, graduate from high school at higher rates, and are more likely to enroll in higher education than students with less involved families. For these reasons, increasing family involvement in the education of their children is an important goal for schools, particularly those serving low-income and other students at risk of failure. (p. 3)

Despite an accumulating body of research demonstrating that parental involvement is linked with better educational outcomes, it is not known what specific types of parental

Ballen, J., & Moles, O. (1994). *Strong families, strong schools*. New York: Columbia University, ERIC Clearinghouse on Urban Education. Retrieved February 25, 2003 from www.eric-web.tc.columbia.edu. Washington, DC: U.S. Department of Education. (ERIC Document Reproduction Service No.)

Beach Center on Disability. (2000a). *How to deliver services to Asian families who have children with disabilities*. Lawrence, KS: University of Kansas.

Beach Center on Disability. (2000b). *How to deliver services to Hispanic families who have children with disabilities*. Lawrence, KS: University of Kansas.

Beach Center on Disability. (2000c). *How to deliver services to Native American families who have children with disabilities*. Lawrence, KS: University of Kansas.

Carey, N., Lewis, L., & Farris, E. (1998). *Parent involvement in children's education: Efforts by public elementary schools* (Report No. NCES 98-032). [National Center for Education Statistics Statistical Analysis Report]. Washington, DC: National Center for Education Statistics. (ERIC Document Reproduction Service No. 416027)

Coontz, S. (1992). *The way we never were: American families and the nostalgia trap*. New York: Basic Books.

Coontz, S. (1997). *The way we really are: Coming to terms with America's changing families*. New York: Basic Books.

Dettmer, P., Dyck, N., & Thurston, L. P. (2002). *Consultation, collaboration, and teamwork for students with special needs* (4th ed.). Boston: Allyn & Bacon.

Dunst, C. J., Trivette C. M., & Deal, A. G. (1994). Final thoughts concerning adoption of family-centered intervention practices. In C. J. Dunst, C. M. Trivette, & A. G. Deal (Eds.), *Supporting and strengthening families: Methods, strategies and practices* (pp. 222–225). Cambridge, MA: Brookline Books.

Dunst, C. J., Trivette, C. M., & LaPointe, N. (1994). Meaning and key characteristics of empowerment. In C. J. Dunst, C. M. Trivette, & A. G. Deal (Eds.), *Supporting and strengthening families: Methods, strategies and practices* (pp. 12–28). Cambridge, MA: Brookline Books.

Edwards, A., & Warin, J. (1999). Parental involvement in raising the achievement of primary school pupils: Why bother? *Oxford Review of Education, 25*(3), 325–341.

Epstein, J. L. (1995). School/family/community partnerships: Caring for the children we share. *Phi Delta Kappan, 76*, 701–712.

Epstein, J. L., & Lee, S. (1995). National patterns of school and family connections in the middle grades. In B. A. Ryan, G. R. Adams, T. P. Gullotta, R. P. Weissberg, & R. L. Hampton (Eds.), *The family–school connection: Theory, research, and practice* (pp. 109–154). Thousand Oaks, CA: Sage.

Friend, M. (2003). *Interactions: Collaboration skills for school professionals* (4th ed.). Boston: Allyn & Bacon.

Funkhouser, J. E., & Gonzales, M. R. (1997). *Family involvement in children's education, successful local approaches.* Idea Book Series. Washington, DC: Office of Educational Research and Improvement, National Institute on the Education of At-Risk Students. Retrieved May 30, 2003, from www.ed.gov/pubs/FamInvolve

Glick, P. C. (1997). Demographic pictures of African American families. In H. P. McAdoo (Ed.), *Black families* (3rd ed., pp. 118–138). Thousand Oaks, CA: Sage.

Gore, A., & Gore, T. (2002). *Joined at the heart: The transformation of the American family.* New York: Henry Holt & Co.

Inger, M. (1992, August). *Increasing the school involvement of Hispanic parents.* ERIC Clearinghouse on Urban Education Digest No. 80 (Report No. EDO-UD-92-3). New York: Columbia University. (ERIC Document Reproduction Service No. ED350380). Retrieved May 29, 2003, from eric-web.tc.columbia.edu

Johnson, H. P., & O'Brien-Strain, M. (2000, November). Underlying population trends. In *Getting to know the future customers of the Office of Child Support: Projections report for 2004 and 2009* (chap. 4). Retrieved March 5, 2003, from www.acf.dhhs.gov/ programs/cse/pubs/reports/projections

Lopez, G. R. (2001). *On whose terms? Understanding involvement through the eyes of migrant parents.* Paper presented at the Annual Meeting of the American Educational Research Association, Seattle, WA. Abstract retrieved January 30, 2003, from www.sedl.org/connections/resources

Lopez, G. R., Scribner, J. D., & Mahitivanichcha, K. (2001). Redefining parental involvement: Lessons from high-performing migrant-impacted schools. *American Educational Research Journal, 38*(2), 253-288.

National Coalition for Parent Involvement in Education, (n.d.). *A framework for family involvement.* Retrieved May 29, 2003, from www.ncpie.org/DevelopingPartnerships

Nord, C. W., & West, J. (2001, May). *Fathers' and mothers' involvement in their children's schools by family type and resident status* (NCES 2001-032). Washington, DC: National Center for Educational Statistics. Retrieved January 30, 2003, from nces.ed.gov/pubsearch/index.asp

Pennsylvania Farm Bureau. (2002). *Pennsylvania agricultural information.* Retrieved March 3, 2003, from www.pfb.com/news/aginfo.html.

Petr, C. G., & Allen, R. I. (1997). Family-centered professional behavior: Frequency and importance to parents. *Journal of Emotional and Behavioral Disorders, 5*(4), 196–204.

Rank, M. R. (2000). Poverty and economic hardship in families. In D. H. Demo, K. R. Allen, & M. A. Fine (Eds.), *Handbook of family diversity* (pp. 293–315). New York: Oxford University Press.

Rivers, R. M., & Scanzoni, J. (1997). Social families among African Americans: Policy implications for children. In H. P. McAdoo (Ed.), *Black families* (3rd ed., pp. 333–348). Thousand Oaks, CA: Sage.

Robbins, R. (2002). The use of traditional American Indian stories and symbols in counseling adolescents with behavioral problems. *Beyond Behavior, 12*(1), 12–19.

Savin-Williams, R. C., & Esterberg, K. G. (2000). Lesbian, gay, and bisexual families. In D. H. Demo, K. R. Allen , & M. A. Fine (Eds.), *Handbook of family diversity* (pp. 197–215). New York: Oxford University Press.

Scott-Jones, D. (1995). Parent–child interactions and school achievement. In B. A. Ryan, G. R. Adams, T. P. Gullotta, R. P. Weissberg, & R. L. Hampton (Eds.), *The family–school connection: Theory, research, and practice* (pp. 75–107). Thousand Oaks, CA: Sage.

Shumow, L., & Miller, J. D. (2001). Parents' at-home and at-school academic involvement with young adolescents. *Journal of Early Adolescence, 21*(1), 68–91.

Sudarkasa, N. (1997). African American families and family values. In H. P. McAdoo (Ed.), *Black families* (3rd ed., pp. 9–40). Thousand Oaks, CA: Sage.

Swap, S. M. (1993). *Developing home–school partnerships: From concepts to practice.* New York: Teachers College Press.

Taylor, R. L. (2000). Diversity within African American families. In D. H. Demo, K. R. Allen, & M. A. Fine (Eds.), *Handbook of family diversity* (pp. 232–251). New York: Oxford University Press.

Trivette, P., & Anderson, E. (1995). The effects of four components of parental involvement on eighth grade student achievement. *School Psychology Review, 24*(2), 299–317.

Truelsen, S. (1999, October 25). *Agriculture is growing. Voice of Agriculture.* Retrieved March 3, 2003, from www.fb.org/views/focus/fo99

Turnbull, A. P., & Turnbull, H. R. (2001). *Families, professionals, and exceptionality: Collaborating for empowerment* (4th ed.). Upper Saddle River, NJ: Merrill/Prentice Hall.

Turnbull, A. P., & Turnbull, H. R., Shank, M., & Leal, D. (1995). *Exceptional lives: Special education in today's schools.* Upper Saddle River, NJ: Merrill/Prentice Hall.

U.S. Census Bureau (2000, December 19). *Table A-2. Percent of People 25 Years Old and over who have completed high school or college, by race, Hispanic Origin and sex: Selected Years 1940 to 2000.* Retrieved January 12, 2003, from www.census.gov/population/socdemo/education/tableA-2.txt

U.S. Census Bureau (2001, September). *Households and families: 2000.* Census 2000 Brief. Retrieved January 12, 2003, from www.census.gov/prod/2001pubs/c2kbro1-8.pdf

U.S. Census Bureau (2002, March 28). *How the nation has changed since the 1930 census.* Retrieved January 12, 2003, from www.census.gov/pubinfo/www/1930_factsheet.html

U.S. Department of Education (2001). *Twenty-third annual report to Congress on the implementation of the Individuals with Disabilities Education Act.* Washington, DC: Author.

White-Clark, R., & Decker, L. E. (1996). *The "hard-to-reach" parent: Old challenges, new insights.* Houston, TX: Decker and Associates. Retrieved May 29, 2003, from eric-web.tc.columbia.edu

Zinn, M. B., & Wells, B. (2000). Diversity within Latino families: New lessons for family social science. In D. H. Demo, K. R. Allen, & M. A. Fine (Eds.), *Handbook of family diversity* (pp. 232–251). New York: Oxford University Press.

Part Two

Case Study Analysis

CHAPTER THREE

Climbing the Mountain: Mr. Derstrom's Story

Commentary: Mr. Derstrom's story provides insight into one father's feelings upon the birth of a son with Down syndrome and his progression through school. Mr. Derstrom, his wife, and his two sons enjoyed strong family support; however, this 37-year-old White man relates how he still struggled with his own sadness and low expectations. In addition, he discusses other sources his family drew upon for support.

Mr. Derstrom talks about the teachers' commitment and care, as well as what he learned from their approaches and the emotional impact of communications with teachers. His story provides an opportunity to discuss the sources of support and the various interpretations of parents' adjustment to having a child with disabilities. Mr. Derstrom's story also raises questions about specific supports for fathers of children with disabilities.

HELPLESSNESS

I'll never forget that first day of November. It was 3 days after one of the best days of my life, the day my younger son was born. I received a phone call at work from my wife saying that the doctor wanted to talk to us before Jonathan was dismissed. The tone of her voice was disturbing, so I drove with haste to the hospital. I don't remember even seeing anyone as I made my way to the room.

If you can imagine having every drop of life-giving, hope-filled, "what-a-great-world-this-is" energy drained from your body in a matter of less than a minute, then you can appreciate the emotions churning within me. Just what is Down syndrome? What is low muscle tone? slow to learn? retarded? Trisomy 21? Just take him home and love him, they say.

> Professionals are often caught in a dilemma to provide adequate factual information to parents, and yet to not overwhelm them. Mr. Derstrom obviously desired more information than was provided on this occasion.

I didn't know what to do. I went to the library. I looked in the card catalog for the reference material on mental retardation, Down syndrome, disabilities, etcetera. I had never been in this section before. I had looked up volumes in the "other" sections of the library, but never here. Was anyone looking? It was early afternoon, and I was reading about these subjects when I should be at work. If I saw anyone I knew, and that was highly likely since this was a small town, they might wonder. They might ask questions that I didn't want to answer.

Well, I did see a neighbor lady there, and of course she asked if the baby had come yet. I confided in her, and she said that she would help in any way possible. We always knew she was nice, but we had never "needed" her. She said to learn all we could about Jonathan's condition...that it would help both him and us.

It's funny, but looking back now it seems that it should have been harder than it was to tell my parents, brother, sister, and all my wife's family that we now have a "special" child in the family. Perhaps my subconscious knew that they would be there for support. I'm not sure how the words came out, but they did, and everyone cried with us.

I planted a tree when my first son, Chad, was born. The seedling had sprung up from seeds that had blown into my parents' yard. Why waste this perfectly good tree? Soon the tree grew to the same height as Chad. I took pictures to record the progress both were making. Both were nurtured so they wouldn't perish. They weathered trial without breaking. They were a joy to behold. The tree and Chad. Why didn't I believe that Jonathan could grow, bend without breaking, flourish despite hardship, and be a thing of greatness and source of pride? We moved away from that town when Jonathan was about 10 months old. I still drive by that house whenever fate takes me there. The tree is tall, full of strong, healthy branches and beautiful to behold. Just like Jonathan.

JUST A BLUR

I took much for granted when watching our first son, Chad, grow up. Learning seemed so natural to him. He learned to read by age 3, could memorize stories and the names of his favorite basketball players, and catch on to things with great ease. Perhaps too well. I failed to notice how easily he was raised. I surely was not prepared for the challenge of raising a child with a disability. Thank God for my wife. She seemed much more prepared for the task ahead. Being a physical therapist, she knew how to prepare Jonathan for the challenges of low muscle tone, weak neck vertebrae, or just being able to grasp objects. How many things passed by me in preparing for this child, but no one is ever prepared for this. What had we done to have this happen? It wasn't our fault, right? Blame and guilt were in the forefront of our thoughts. Perhaps knowing that this birth was just an accident of nature helped somewhat, but at the time, not much. Faith is especially important at a time like this. I knew we had greatness in our arms, but I didn't imagine that I would be able to have the pride in Jonathan that I had in Chad. How wrong I was!

Older people have always said that time goes more quickly as you grow older. Maybe I had aged faster than my years during Jonathan's first 4 years, but they are now just a blur in my memory. I remember the sympathy of friends and the statements such as, "He will be the most loving child," "God didn't do this to you; He is crying with you," and "Special children are only born to parents that can handle it." Well, I wasn't one of those parents. I didn't know I could handle it. I had always learned to hold my emotions inside and take care of my own concerns without help. This event, however, brought out the emotions of heartache, fear of the future, and probably the emotion of feeling sorry for myself. That emotion didn't help, but simply created another hurdle to jump.

We had tremendous support and acceptance of friends and family, for the most part. We were fortunate to be part of a loving family; one that cried with us, but never turned away or blamed us for having a child with Down syndrome. Baby gifts were just like those of "normal" kids. My mother always helped and cheered on the underdog. The journey to acceptance of Jonathan was nil, and Jonathan soon became Grandma's "Angel." My dad was ready to do anything. He was immediately protective of Jonathan, and was always on the verge of giving a tongue-lashing to anyone who said anything bad. All the family was willing to baby-sit anytime needed. Jonathan was about 2 months old when he was held for the first time by my grandmother, his great-grandma. She took one look at him and said he was "just fine…nothing wrong with him." I knew this wasn't true, but just Grandma protecting him. I wanted to laugh and cry at the same time. Dealing with reality was tough.

MOUNTAIN PEAKS

Women may be able to verbalize their feelings at difficult times better than men. We all want to protect our kids from harm…perhaps dads more than moms in cases like this. I didn't know what to say, so much of the time I said nothing. I do remember so many thoughts racing through my mind as to Jonathan's future that talking to someone else was impossible. I was caught up within myself. Enjoying the miracles of each day is possible now, but living one day at a time was impossible then.

I didn't think I would ever have to know what happens within the walls of a developmental preschool, but it proves that even I could learn something. He wasn't quite 4 years old the fall of his first day of school. It was a day that would prove to be scary, painful, heart-warming and most of all, wonderful. His schoolbag was packed just like any normal boy on the first day of this journey into life. It must have weighed about 10 pounds. Jonathan handled it like the warrior he has turned out to be. Walking was difficult, partly under the weight of the bag, partly because it hit him in the back of the knees, or maybe partly because he knew he was departing on a long journey. The bottom of the bag was only a few inches from the ground. Too bad I didn't see more clearly how tall and strong he actually stood. The bag was heavy, not his spirit. I'm sure that he didn't know what was ahead, but he climbed the mountain better than I did. Yes, it seemed like an overwhelming peak to me. I had the privilege of knowing someone during my life that used to say that there was "no hill too high for a climber." I guess Jonathan has become quite a climber.

CORN?

Mrs. Trudy, Jonathan's teacher, has been through the first day of school many times. She had introduced special children to the world of learning for years. Everyone was important. Perhaps you could talk, perhaps not. Maybe you could walk, maybe not. Lunchtime had to be quite an adventure. It had never occurred to me that the colors in the room were important to the learning process. Textures, smells, bright colors, and all the sensory experiences were vital. In the middle of all this mixture was a child-size swimming pool filled with corn. What if he sits in it, I thought? What if it gets in his pants pockets? What if he pours it over his head? Well, all those things happened, and it was great! I learned how important it was for Jonathan to experience learning by touch and feel. Hugs help a lot too. He learned a lot all right. It was a good thing I wasn't the teacher.

How protective parents are with their children. Normal kids have difficulty, but somehow we work through the down days knowing they can handle it. They are normal kids, right? Somehow, trust in the ability of these special children to cope is more difficult to develop. Who will protect them? Can I shelter Jonathan from all harm like a good father should? I had never even thought that a child would not develop a sense of danger. He thought nothing of running out into the street or walking in front of the swings on the playground. More importantly, he would give anything to a stranger, not even thinking about it being lost or not returned. He trusts everyone. He loves everyone. He can't imagine doing something bad to another on purpose. Perhaps Jonathan's trust was something he taught to me. At least I'm trying to learn.

One of the things I learned during those first years of school was that we should never forget the effect we can have on someone else. Mrs. Trudy told us that she suspected our son had autistic tendencies. "Based on what?" I asked. Well, he seemed to be able to

> How could the preschool teacher have expressed her concerns in a way that would not have hurt Mr. Derstrom?

shut out the attention of others, he seemed preoccupied, he seemed too involved in himself, too much with watching a movie rather than experiencing outside influences in his life. Having a son with Down syndrome seemed enough to deal with right now. But, autism, too? That was more load than any child should have to bear. This diagnosis had better be more than a guess! Nothing proved to be true in regard to autism. It was a quick judgment and a thought stated out loud, without thinking of our devastation.

I was relieved that no more burden was placed on Jonathan. As kind-hearted as that teacher was, I'll never forget how insensitive that statement was to me.

HOPE

Inclusion was a foreign word to me before Jonathan. When I was growing up, special education was for the outcasts of education. A place to put kids when they couldn't learn. Looking back, some of those people (some my own age) didn't belong there. They were the products of broken homes, lack of positive influences, praise, friends and a system that wouldn't give them a chance. Prejudices were rampant. No one was reaching out to include them in life as a normal child. How far our educational system has come! Too bad some things come from being forced upon us, instead of being willingly accepted as progress. If we could display that helpfulness and caring for others through our own initiative, without being forced upon us, how neat! I want Jonathan's teachers to include him because they want to without a second thought, not because inclusion was forced on them. Governmental mandates work, but at what price?

There is a song that says, "faith, hope, and love. And the greatest of these is love." I'm not so sure. Hope is the reason to get up in the morning. Hope that today will bring another word of encouragement, another small step towards accomplishment, and another brick added to the structure of this wonderful person known as my "handicapped" child. We have been blessed with wonderful, caring teachers who live this and don't leave it at the school's threshold when the clock says you may leave. They have treated Jonathan as an individual; had him develop his skills beyond what I would have asked of him. And always, they gave him the love he so easily showed to them. This is not a story of educational roadblocks, uncaring administrators, apathy, and lack of encouragement. What a difference it must make. We are so lucky.

TOO MUCH HUGGING?

We have always had the goal of helping Jonathan be as socially acceptable as possible because society looks down on "those children." They are the handicapped kids who don't look or act "normal." Reality sets in pretty quickly when you have a special child. A child that will have enough challenges to break the will of most people. He may not have the most expensive clothes, but he is always dressed in the kids' current style. He has a nice haircut and is always clean and rested for school.

It seems ironic that Jonathan is liked so much that a new challenge has evolved. In the third grade, Jonathan developed a circle of friends, mostly girls in his grade, who wanted to help him too much. He can put on his own boots, zip his coat, find his locker, and carry his bookbag. The help extended to being good friends and usually meant a big hug each morning as they greeted one another at school. Teachers were not immune from this ritual either, but we all realized that, sadly, all this hugging wasn't appropriate. You see, hugging isn't socially acceptable behavior in this area of the country. Even between family, kisses and hugs are rare. Jonathan displayed his love unconditionally and was just unaware that it was inappropriate. This was a tough lesson to learn (especially for the teachers). We had to teach Jonathan other types of greetings, like a handshake or high five. Eventually, with daily reminders, these actions became common, and hugs were reserved for family.

LEARNING A FOREIGN LANGUAGE

Spanish, German, French. These were the foreign languages available to me during my days in school. I never took advantage of the opportunity to learn a foreign language. I regretted missing the chance and thought that it was gone forever until my special child was born. When Jonathan entered school, I was given my opportunity to learn a foreign language, but not a language offered in my days.

"Staffings" was a term I never knew until the school life of Jonathan developed. This, I found out, is an opportunity for all the persons involved in my child's education and training to meet and discuss past progress and develop future goals. It happens about two times per year and is very useful, especially for the providers of the education. My first experience at a staffing was confusing and did not seem to involve me as a parent. My wife and I are considered to be very supportive and involved parents with the educational process. However, this first staffing was not as I expected. The teacher, aides, and therapists are all good people, but it seemed to me that I should have been an integral part of this meeting. They talked to each other in this foreign tongue that was gratifying to them but unknown to me. During His earthly life, Jesus was able to have everyone hear the words of the Galilean prophets in his own tongue. That miracle is not yet possible for teachers.

> This comment may provide you with a clue about another important source of support for Mr. Derstrom.

Terminology reduced to abbreviations such as WISC, MMPI, DST, HELP, CA, AA, and the dreaded Stanford Binet, meant volumes to the persons present at the meeting, but it meant nothing to me. After listening for what seemed to be an hour to the developmental assessment of my Jonathan discussed in this foreign language, and having to slowly feel my legs fall asleep after sitting in that child-size chair for the same length of time, my patience was gone. The group had excluded us long enough.

I am sure my temper showed when I finally spoke up and asked for a report in my own language. I was probably more sarcastic than angry sounding. My response seemed quite surprising to the staff, but we all were much more at ease when this revelation came to be known. I'm sure it helped that they knew we were a part of the team and not of a "we versus them" mentality. We all got quite a laugh and a valuable lesson was learned. I have since learned some of this foreign language and will never forget my first day at this school.

THE NEXT CHAPTER

Middle school poses a challenge for normal kids. The changing environment of a new school building, some new classmates, new teachers, and moving between rooms causes anxiety for all. However, the anxiety can be greatly diminished when you are received with enthusiasm and a "can-do" attitude. This is the next stepping-stone in the path of Jonathan's classroom future.

We met with the administration of the middle school to reduce the tension that this new venture is causing my wife and I. We hoped to hear how they plan to adapt to my son and to verbally "lay down the law" about my expectations towards Jonathan's educational future. I am tougher in my own mind than I am in reality. Happily, I soon learned that the school feels Jonathan will be a valuable asset in his classrooms. To prepare Jonathan, he was encouraged to visit the new school without us, and he quickly learned the names of his new teachers, the areas of the building, the names of the school secretaries, etcetera. He doesn't seem to be worried about this new challenge. He told us that the new principal, the secretaries, and the teachers were looking forward to having him there. He seems proud of this fact. We all hugged and breathed a collective sigh of relief.

> From where does the term *inclusion student* originate? What is the implication of this terminology?

We asked the principal about the attitude of the teachers in having an inclusion student with them. We have to remember that this will not be the first time for a special-needs student to be with them. His gratifying response was that his main teacher and the others actually had asked for Jonathan to be in their classes. Good for them, good for him, good for us.

THANK-YOU

It will perhaps seem redundant to discuss the love and acceptance that has always been shown to my son in the school community at large. The fear and apprehension that occupied so much of my time has greatly diminished with the years of support given to Jonathan by others. Pride, wonder, love, surprise, closeness…all are terms to describe the emotions I have experienced in watching him develop along with the "welcome" he is given every day by our educational community. There have been some stones along the way upon which we have tripped, but never a stone that couldn't be rolled aside to reveal the great wonder of his ability to learn. It is extremely important to note that opportunities have always been provided to Jonathan beyond my own expectations. This is a great gift offered by those who have taught my son. They did not see a boy that has limitations. They did not pass him by or give up. Yes, they had to adapt to some special circumstances, but they never said, "Let's not try." Those that can touch the life of another in such a way are truly gifted. I am sure that not enough "thank-yous" have been said along the way. I know he has also touched others when I hear teachers request his inclusion in their classroom. They shed as many tears of joy as we do when success, in whatever small way, is achieved. Hugs are given even if he is not supposed to learn those behaviors in school.

I recognize the true value of an accepting, loving, caring, never-say-die teacher. So does Jonathan. He may not look you in the eye and make you believe your importance to him, but he knows your worth. It is for that and a system that says "welcome" that this long overdue and sincere "thank-you" is offered to all those who have touched my son and for all those who are called to the life of an educator. Remember that parents can forget your worth, at times, but they will never forget when you accept and defend the challenges the "special" children of this world can overcome. Thank-you!

Activities

1. Briefly summarize the main points that you believe contributed to the generally successful experiences this family has had in collaborating with the schools. What does Mr. Derstrom say about this?

2. Compile two lists: (a) list everything that teachers or administrators have done that Mr. Derstrom would consider "best practice" and (b) list everything that teachers or administrators have done that Mr. Derstrom would consider "bad practice."

3. Relate the various feelings indicated or implied by this father to the theoretical descriptions of feelings that parents display as they learn to cope with their child's disability.

4. Determine Mr. Derstrom's most apparent sources of support and compare these to the sources of support discussed in professional literature. Did he indicate a need for additional support and, if so, do you see a source of support that he and his wife overlooked or that may not have been available?

5. *Discuss:* First, assess Mr. Derstrom's potential to take on a broader leadership role in educational matters that concern other children or policy issues. Then, discuss the ways that you, as a teacher or principal, could mentor Mr. Derstrom and/or his wife to further develop their leadership capabilities and the factors that might inhibit Mr. Derstrom from developing this role.

6. How could the principal and teachers put Mr. and Mrs. Derstrom at ease about sending Jonathan to middle school? Role-play the meeting they had before his first day.

7. Mr. Derstrom describes how much he learned from Mrs. Trudy about his son's educational needs. Design a series of parent workshops for Mr. Derstrom and the other preschoolers' parents or the parents of the children in your own class. What topics would you choose? What structure would you use? What variables and assumptions would influence your design process? Develop an agenda for one session.

8. Mr. Derstrom discusses how hard it was for him to talk about his feelings and the differences he sees in the way men and women share their emotions and cope. After a search of the professional literature, support or refute what Mr. Derstrom said. What are the suggested strategies for meeting the needs of fathers?

9. We have some insight into Mr. Derstrom's preference for knowledge acquisition through reading because the first thing he did upon learning of his son's diagnosis was to go to the library to read about Down syndrome. Because Mr. Derstrom expressed a struggle against overprotecting Jonathan, put together a reading packet for Mr. Derstrom on the importance of and the strategies to foster a child's independence.

10. Role-play the IEP meeting that Mr. Derstrom described as containing jargon, which caused him to feel left out. One person should play the role of a team member whose duty is to ensure the family's ideas are heard and their needs are addressed. Practice how this individual could intervene on behalf of Mr. Derstrom. Consider what signs Mr. Derstrom might show and how the advocate might intervene with the team to raise awareness of the effect of their behavior and language.

11. Research your local area to find a support group that might be appropriate for Mr. Derstrom.

12. As Mrs. Trudy, write a letter to all of your students' parents that explains your use of developmentally appropriate practices, such as playing in corn.

13. Interview the parent or grandparent of a child with disabilities to learn their feelings about the diagnosis of their child. Ask them to discuss how their feelings changed over time, what factors influenced their adaptation, and whether professionals gave them the desired level of hope.

14. *Discuss:* Is Mr. Derstrom overly protective of Jonathan? How can teachers help parents foster independence?

15. *Discuss:* How do you feel about the mandates for change that Mr. Derstrom discusses as unfortunate but necessary? Do you think Mr. Derstrom could tell if a teacher had volunteered or had been forced to include his child?

16. Describe the best practices that teachers and other helping professionals should use to assist this family.

17. Write an analysis of this case, drawing parallels from this case to (a) your own experiences; (b) theory and research from class discussions, course readings, and knowledge gained in previous classes; and (c) other cases in this book.

Suggested Resources

Ferguson, P. M. (2002). A place in the family: An historical interpretation of research on parental reactions to having a child with a disability. *Journal of Special Education, 36*(3), 124–130, 147.

Meyer, D. (1995). *Uncommon fathers: Reflections on raising a child with a disability.* Bethesda, MD: Woodbine House.

Naseef, R. A. (2001). *The struggles and rewards of raising a child with a disability.* Baltimore: Paul H. Brookes.

Summer, J. A., Behr, S. K., & Turnbull, A. P. (1989). Positive adaptation and coping strengths of families who have children with disabilities. In G. H. S. Singer and L. Irvin (Eds.), *Support for care-giving families: Enabling positive adaptations to disability* (pp. 27–40). Baltimore: Paul H. Brookes.

Online Resources

Visit the Web site of the National Down Syndrome Society at http://www.ndss.org for information on resources.

Also visit the Web site of the Fathers Network at http:// www.fathersnetwork.org for resources for fathers of children with disabilities.

CHAPTER FOUR

I Made Myself High Profile: Bright Star's Story

Commentary: Bright Star is the Native American mother of three grown biological children and three adopted children who are now teenagers. She is 57 years old and has been single for the past 10 years. This is Bright Star's story of Jim, an Apache and Hispanic child adopted at 10 months. Jim is hearing impaired and has learning disabilities. Bright Star has not always been satisfied with the quality of Jim's education, and she challenges professionals to consider whether they make use of the knowledge that a parent has to share.

Bright Star is an outspoken community activist, particularly regarding American Indian affairs, and this foreshadows how she will approach conflicts with schools. She confronts problems head-on, she is persistent, and she does not let little things "slide." Bright Star explains that she grabs control of what she can to make a statement. She has also taught Jim to stand up for what he considers right, and you will see how he reflects this teaching in school. This case provides an opportunity to discuss how a parent's activism might make educators uncomfortable. It also reflects a parental advocacy that is accompanied by a sense of humor and pride in her children.

HOW JIM CAME TO BE WITH US

My son, Jim Little Bear, is a Native American/Hispanic child that we adopted at 10 1/2 months. According to the available information, his birth mother was a 21-year-old Apache and Hispanic woman living in the Southwest. He was born prematurely in a hospital, weighing in at 4 pounds and 1/4 ounce. He spent approximately 6 weeks in their care and, according to the birth mother, he was not supposed to live. Her knowledge of what, exactly, was wrong with him was limited—he could not swallow and choked. He also has a cut-down scar on his right ankle, indicating a long-term drip treatment of some kind.

Jim was released to his biological mother's care at about 5 pounds. Due to her economic situation and lack of understanding as to what was needed for such a tiny infant, he soon developed a bronchial infection and breathing problems. His illness was apparent to the owners of a restaurant his biological mother frequented, and they called the Department of Social Services. Both mother and child were taken into custody and hospitalized, as she, too, was ill. Upon release from the hospital, Jim was placed in foster care. A social worker, with translating staff, worked with her to try to establish a workable, single parent situation. He was 2 1/2 months old.

During the ensuing 7 1/2 months, he was with other foster children in an environment that was very loving and hands-on. He had ongoing ear infections and colds, but began to gain weight, and he became very socialized.

At 10 months, we adopted him. My husband was a retired military officer, well-established in a second career with a corporation. He had biological children, but due to family circumstances and the military career, he had not parented them past the age of preschool. I was in my early 40s, and had successfully raised three biological children who were now out of the home. I had hoped to have a larger family, but it had not worked out. I am Native American, of the Delaware tribe, and am very aware of the need for stable homes for minority children. We were both well-educated, had an upper-middle-class income, and able to provide long term. I believed firmly in at-home parenting, was an active community participant, with a wide range of acquaintances, friends, and relatives.

BONDING, THRIVING, AND ANTIBIOTICS

When Jim came to us, he was declared physically well and free of infections, with a tendency to "otitis media," which with caution and care, he would probably outgrow. He was believed to be developmentally delayed, with failure to thrive and lack of maternal bonding. He weighed 13 pounds at this time, was fine boned and a finicky eater. He rarely slept all night, and was on a bottle.

> Otitis media is an inflammation of the middle ear and is common in young children. It can result in conductive hearing loss and speech and language delays when a child has frequent episodes.

His bonding to me was nearly instant, to the point that when I put him down on the motel bed while I went into the bathroom, he screamed, cried, and attempted to scuttle to the bed's edge to get to me. Once, however, my husband lifted him and set him at my feet in the bathroom, he was instantly calmed. He hasn't changed much since!

Within 4 weeks of living with us, Jim had gained weight so quickly as to be almost unrecognizable. He ate anything put in front of him. He began such activities as climbing, walking around hanging on to things, and by 12 months walked without support. He slept well at night, took a long afternoon nap, and played with his pets. There is a cute photo of him crawling after the cat at full speed.

During this time he had an ongoing ear infection that was treated continuously by a pediatrician. Jim was talking, saying words such as cookie, light, kitty cat. He had been treated immediately for this ongoing infection, so I questioned the doctor about why the continuing antibiotics failed to keep him infection free. The standard response was that he was cutting teeth, that I was overly concerned, etcetera. I told him that I had raised three children, with none of this; they all got teeth just fine. The pediatrician advised me to leave the doctoring to him.

Jim's physical progress seemed excellent. He was agile and very tactile. Anything Jim saw someone do, he could emulate with apparent ease. His balance and speed was often a cause for comment. The fact that he was an adorable looking child, with a disposition that drew people to him, added to this, and exposed him to the attentions and affection of many people.

DEAFNESS

At 25 months, Jim had a particularly bad bout of the ear infection, which the doctor was going to treat over the phone. In disgust, I took Jim to another pediatrician. This doctor was concerned, and said that Jim had distorted, inflamed, and ruptured eardrums. This was the first that I had heard of this. She also gave Jim an overall physical, in which he displayed some delay in basic testing (with blocks, etc.). He had also stopped talking. An immediate appointment was made for 4 days later with a specialist at a nearby hospital.

> From Bright Star's perspective, what lesson could be learned from this experience? Consider how this early experience might influence Bright Star's trust of professionals.

Microscopic examination and evaluation produced the verdict that Jim was deaf and had literally no eardrums left. That was why he had stopped talking. They tested to determine the loss, he was fitted with hearing aids, and arrangements were made to take him to a speech therapy clinic. All of this was accomplished in less than a month. During this time it was learned Jim was adept at reading lips and making judgment calls as to what was needed or wanted by facial expression and tone of voice.

For about a year from that time, Jim saw the speech therapist twice weekly, with one-on-one treatment. He was also totally infection free. He wore his hearing aid without problems, although he was quick to pull the battery out and put it down. Many times I would have him go get it in the dark! He always knew exactly where it was! His speech improved at an acceptable rate. Being a very vocal person, I talked constantly to him, and was with him 24 hours a day. Also being a social person involved in varying activities with People, Jim was continually exposed to speech, conversation, words, and inflection. Jim was also given a Walkman and headset to hear stories and music on. The first time he put it on, with his oldest sister, the look on his face was pure delight and joy.

With a hearing-impaired child at such a young age, you have to wonder what they get and what they miss. Driving cross-country, changing from one highway to another outside of St. Louis, the voice emanating from the car-seat on the passenger side, with a finger pointing, asked, "Donal's Mommy, Donal's." I said, "In a few minutes, Jim, this is a hard road here, with too many cars—we'll stop later." Jim said very emphatically, "Mommy, Donal's, now!" I took my eyes off the traffic long enough to look his way, to see what he saw. I laughed all the way through St. Louis! Jim had seen the huge St. Louis Arch, and must have thought it was the McDonald's to end all McDonald's.

FINDING NEW SERVICES

Jim was 3 when we moved to the eastern seaboard. With a new location, house, and acoustics, it was fall before Jim was once again enrolled in speech therapy. It was here that some problems began. The new program did not want to accept the testing from the previous state, even though all bills, etcetera. had been paid by private insurance and us. Their treatment of Jim as a person was less hands-on or caring. The teacher and director involved did not attempt to establish any rapport or individual contact with Jim. The one woman was more bent on impressing me with her credentials and how busy she was.

> Can you offer another interpretation for the teacher's behavior?

Their tone of voice with both me and Jim was abrupt, down the nose, and brusque. The "teacher" woman was short and impatient with Jim, and when I called her on this, she informed me that she usually didn't work with children this young and wouldn't be his permanent teacher. Jim reverted to accidents, although he had been toilet trained for sometime. He also did NOT want to go to the speech classes. They were not one-on-one, but done in a small group. After some fruitless and frustrating sessions and letters with those in charge, I removed him temporarily.

A program for children with disabilities which ran in conjunction with the regular school programs was recommended. Jim was eligible when he was 4 1/2. He is a January child, so he could not enter regular kindergarten, anyway. He spent 2 years in this program, going half days. He did exceptionally well, and I was assured that he was ready for regular school. They said that he had more difficulty with math, but he would do OK.

During this period, he was also enrolled in a Montessori-based preschool. Montessori method is supposedly noted for its hands-on, touchy-feely type of education geared to the individual child, which is why I chose to go the extra expense. It was the director's first year in business—the building had just been finished. I soon noted that she was more worried about the children ruining her new facilities than about the education of the children. When one of the teacher's assistants left the employ of the school, she called me and told me that Jim was being ignored due to the "problem" children that were enrolled and were real "pains." Jim, being the child he was—no trouble at all, just got passed right over. He was given no time or real care. The teacher would note in her conferences that Jim couldn't do this or that, and was behind the other children, but always commented on what a big help he was with the other children, in putting things away, and how neat he was. Although the socialization was excellent, he got short shift in being educated due to his manners and ease of fitting in. The teacher also complained a couple times that he hugged other children too much, invading their space. When I would attempt to tell her how best to handle a child with his long-term hearing problems, she brushed it aside as not fitting with her schedules.

The Indian Child Welfare Act of 1978 reestablished tribal authority over the adoption of Native American children. If a child is removed for foster care or adoption, the law requires Native American children be placed with extended family members, other tribal members, or other Native American families. If a child is not living on the reservation, the state must give notice to the child's tribe, wherever the child may be in the United States.

GROWING THE FAMILY

Jim was 4 when we introduced two siblings into the family, a biological sister and brother, ages 3 and 4. They came from the same state and the same State agency as Jim. As with Jim, we relied heavily on their Hispanic origins to ensure no breakdown or later ramifications.

It was only a minor matter, as they had been abandoned or released for adoption by parents who accepted Hispanic identity from the community at large, it being considered preferable to Indian in most cases. Jim's previous foster mom went and observed the two children to ensure that they would fit in with Jim—a family match. They were flown to us with a bilingual social worker. Jim had no problem accepting them. He actually took on the job of being their "big brother," although he is the middle child by 2 months.

As Montessori didn't really work as we'd hoped, all three children were sent to an excellent church preschool 3 afternoons a week. Jim did well artistically, and was much loved and pampered by the teachers there.

Jim followed his new brother by 1 year into school. He went to a mainstream kindergarten class with his sister, who is 9 months younger than he. Jim did fairly well in kindergarten. He wore his aid, and the teacher wore an auditory trainer. He was still infection free. However, it was now that I began to wonder if perhaps Jim might be dyslexic. He had a big tendency to transpose digits and letters, and had problems with fine motor tasks such as writing. I was told it was due to (a) his hearing loss at such a young age and (b) being premature, as low birth weight children take some time to catch up. Any standard testing they did was "nonconclusive." He still had speech therapy.

> What disadvantages affect sa family when children attend different schools? Was this placement change a violation of Jim's right to due process?

After the school promised me that Jim would stay with his siblings, on the same bus, in the same school, they sent him to first grade at another school. Jim's new siblings, naturally close due to the abandonment, turned totally to each other. It was difficult for them to accept Jim. I'd spent 20 months making a threesome out of the two plus one, and succeeded. Then, they separated them! I was informed about a month prior to school starting that the changes had been made, due to busing and availability of the teacher.

NEW SCHOOLS

I had to go along with the new school, under protest, and it was a disaster. Jim knew no one at his new school, and there were different acoustics. They bused him to speech therapy, making it necessary for him to eat lunch en route. He also had a teacher who had no experience with children with hearing impairments, which was not what I had been led to believe. Again, I was dealing with a person who didn't like me telling her anything that was in Jim's testing recommendations or within my realm of experience. She also had problems with Jim being an affectionate child. He was and is always quick to offer a hug to a fallen child, or give his dessert to the child who dropped his.

I was frustrated to the point of tears. I made umpteen phone calls, even involving two university programs in all this. I do NOT trust in school testing, or the results being filed where anyone can get at them. Letters, meetings, protests, and recommendations from the two university programs were useless.

I took about 8 pounds of his school records, and went to the local Catholic school to beg them to take him in their school. They did the next week, and Jim did super well in mainstream first and second grades. He had the same teacher both years, and she was wonderful. She was in her 40s, a dear personality, extremely patient but firm, very hands on, and one-on-one with her class. In second grade, he maintained a *B* average.

Third grade was another disaster. He had a teacher who didn't want her schedule interrupted, told Jim publicly that he was holding back the class, and she didn't like little boys in general. I pulled in the state child advocacy representative, the psychologist that the children and I had been counseling with, and called a general meeting.

They tested Jim for learning disabilities, but again, stated it was nonconclusive. I felt like we were getting no-where. The Catholic school had no services for Jim's problems, and the public school wouldn't address them beyond the classroom. I was still not up to speed on the laws at that time, and was trying to be nice and helpful, and not overbearing. That's not easy for me.

There was this 27-year-old man, who had been at the public school where Jim was, who I hired as a tutor. He was born deaf. His mother was a secretary, I believe, and he had done a project or two with Jim's class. He had called me, worried about what had happened to Jim at the public school. He came out to the house, and we worked out a deal where he would tutor Jim 3 hours a week. He could see at a glance what Jim was not getting, and went so far as to go to Jim's school to attempt to help the teacher. She would accept neither his help nor the suggestions of the psychologist.

At ages 7 and 8, Jim had two major surgeries, tympanoplasties, to rebuild the eardrums in both ears. Both surgeries appeared successful. He was said to have about 85 to 90% hearing, although there was some tonal loss and differentiation.

I had been a single parent since Jim was 6. When he was 10, the family moved to a southern state where my older children and friends resided. Back to square one. The new state would not accept the previous state's 3-month-old testing and recommendations. I've long since learned that the schools get funding "credits" for the amount of minority testing done, and no one wants to pick up where others leave off! They have to jockey for their own pecking order, and the kids be damned. Jim was placed in a mainstream group, and lost ground rapidly. There were new faces, new acoustics, new accents, and no allowance for his problem, even though the new system had been notified and given all the paperwork well in advance of the August start-up date.

> From a school system's perspective, why would a district want to conduct its own testing on a child who moves into the school system?

Finally, after doing their own testing, the same ones that he'd always had, he was put in a special education class. He was one of only two students with hearing impairments, and there was a big age difference, but he had a good teacher. He managed to catch up, but math was horrific. I was positive LD/dyslexia played a part in the ongoing problems. He could do anything orally, or hands-on, but to transfer written words to paper was a lost cause.

HIGHER PROFILE

My battles, to this point, with the committees and powers in charge did little other than frustrate me and cause them to be angered and unhappy with a confrontational mother. I became very vocal in the community. I pulled all his files, dating back to age 2. I made phone calls to the state, to four well-respected universities, to a judge, and to an attorney. I got out articles, and reread all that had been said and done prior to that. I threatened them with the Individuals With Disabilities Education Act. I questioned them in front of each other and quoted their own words back at them. I wrote letters with copies to anyone I could think of who would help, or at least complain about me and my tactics. I was very vocal about having special education teachers with no hearing-impaired experience attempting to educate my son. I sat at meetings of other boards I might be on and moaned about the school system and what they were

> From Bright Star's perspective, why would it be necessary to involve outside authorities and be public about her criticisms?

not doing for my son. In general, I made myself very high profile. I send all the children to school, clean, neat, on time, and eager to learn. So all they have to do is teach. Period. Not a lot to ask.

Jim did receive speech therapy in the school, and the use of an auditory trainer which was not always working or available. He did not wear his aids, because the peripheral sound, the constant attempt to sort and hear what was necessary, and ignore the rest, was very exhausting. I provided Jim with a lap computer that had built-in math programs, reading, and other school items. I was involved in his projects for school, and I continued my own trips, talks, and input with Jim and his siblings.

During this time, Jim also began another round of ear infections, with oozing, and continual antibiotics. He had a "hole" in the right drum again, which would not heal.

Sixth grade was difficult. The teacher was more interested in her volleyball team than the children. I learned that her previous experience was in the prison system, not with special education. Her background for hearing impaired was nil.

In seventh grade, Jim's special ed teacher was herself the parent of a child with severe handicaps. I learned Jim's IEP was NOT being followed at all by his mainstream teachers, a state offense. They were supposed to be doing oral testing, shortened assignments, reading directions, ignoring misspelled words, and giving extended time for in-class work and tests. Two of his mainstream teachers hadn't even bothered to read his IEP. The principal, who has had ongoing problems with many besides me, chose to ignore his IEP, and me, and so instructed a couple teachers. I spoke with an attorney, got some specifics, wrote the state, and the county (after the superintendent had ignored me, also) and sent a copy to the newspaper. It got their attention. I never talk by phone to anyone anymore. I always do it in writing! I'd said I would sue for half a million. They called in their own attorney, who, as it turned out, told them, "She can sue you, and probably will. You had better see to it the child gets all the services he has been promised, or this woman will surely take you to court. And she'll win."

Finally, under threat of court action, testing was done once again. His testing showed him to be 3 years ahead of his age group in vocabulary and understanding. His intonation and speech patterns are quite good, enough so that it is remarked on sometimes that he speaks well for a child who lost hearing at such a young age. A conference was held with the attorney for Jim present. Jim was said to be LD/dyslexic, as well as hearing impaired, which automatically entitles him to all services that the state and system has to offer. After a rather painful start, everything finally settled down, and Jim did quite well overall. He was, as always, well-liked, no problem, very apt to pitch in and help.

He had another major surgery at age 15, a radical right mastoidectomy to correct a massive infection in that bone caused by the ongoing infections. They did another graft to rebuild the nonexistent drum on the right side and straighten out the canal a bit.

His year in eighth grade was terrific. He did special projects, became a peer tutor, helped with the little children in kindergarten and first who have physical and emotional problems. They loved him, as did the teachers. Jim also organized an entire program on his Apache ancestry for family night, with all of us as his display. Although it wasn't highly technical, we were the most visited and talked about program. At his recognition day, he walked off with seven certificates, several gifts, and a trophy, plus the adulation, hugs, and praise of teachers, parents, and kids.

IDENTITY

Everyone kept telling me what a nice boy Jim was, and how well-mannered, sweet and loving, and popular he was. As Native People, we are very involved in Indian country, with some activism. Jim dances in regalia, helps out at Gatherings and other functions, and has no problem at all interacting at length with Elders and other People. The children are very aware of who they are, where they come from, and how they need to proceed.

> Bright Star explains, "I was taught that all tribal groups, in one way or another, referred to themselves as 'the People.' If you hear a Native person speak, you will hear the intonation, the PEOPLE, our PEOPLE."

Jim is the activist of the three, being vocal when he needs to be. He told his fourth grade teacher that he wouldn't do anything for columbus, as murderers don't deserve special treatment, and columbus murdered "his People." He was a dreadful man, so we kind of did our own passive protest—no capital letters for christopher columbus. I mentioned it in passing to someone else, who laughed and not only didn't capitalize cc, she started doing her ex-husband and mother-in-law, too! In a time of violence and loss of self-control, I attempt to give myself, and the children, little things that in our minds exert control and statement.

In fifth grade, at a demographic type exam given to the kids in the gym, Jim raised his hand and said that there was no place for him and his brother and sister on the form, and that his mother told them not to ever check "other." The vice principal, who told me about this, told him it was "number five—Alaskan Natives/Native Americans." Another time, he took a school form to the vice principal and showed him the two blocks "White" and "Black" and politely told him that the form was illegal and offered to bring in the correct one that his mother had just gotten back from Washington!

When things are said in school that aren't correct, like history books, etcetera, he speaks out. I ended up correcting the eighth grade book's chapter on Indians of this state for the teachers, all due to Jim seeing, and saying, "that is NOT right." He took an Indian newspaper into class for a mock election, to show them why one was a better ticket because more Indian issues were being addressed. During one of the testings by an outside PhD at the school, Jim took exception to the man thinking that being an Indian was a lot of fun, and thinking that we all have family on reservations. Sixty percent of this country's Indians are nonreservation, nonfederal, non-card-holding. Jim said he "didn't want to be…what's that big word, Mom?" "Confrontational?" I asked. He told him that, (a) our People on the East coast never had reservations; that is what the government did, and (b) every day isn't a "ball of laughs." One of his classmates this year told me the other day that Jim just rolls his eyes when People say things about Indians that are off-the-wall.

CONCLUSION

At 16, he seems to be physically caught up or catching up—he's 5 feet 6 inches, 114 pounds, long dark hair in a braid, very handsome, perfect teeth, with tons of friends. He runs cross-country, is on the varsity track team, and is said to be a super runner, as is his brother. He, along with his brother, are half way to their black belt in traditional Korean Tae kwon do. The boys have also played baseball and soccer for 2 years, and were in scouts for years. Mark depends on Jim for entrée into social situations, and Jim depends on Mark to make sure that he hears the important stuff.

The three young ones emulate and care greatly for my three grown children, and the relationship is quite close considering the age differences. Their older brother and two sisters are through school and working, and have their own homes. We have contact at long stretches during the summer and all holidays, and through phone calls and involvement with alma maters. The youngest grown girl is often kidded about their pictures being on her desk. My grown son feels that the fact that he and his wife will not have children of their own was meant that way, so he could be around more for these three.

Jim is currently in ninth grade with his siblings, but again, in a new school. He is in special education, and not mainstreamed at this time. He does well on the computer, and uses it at home for projects. At the new school, no one seems to read what gets sent them, and I have had a problem with one teacher already. The computer teacher threatened Jim with in-school suspension because he asks too many questions. That is part of his IEP! I wrote a very civil, explanatory letter, giving her the benefit of the doubt of not knowing that asking questions is part of his program. She told him, in front of the class, that she is stronger than any parent. Any letters she gets, she balls up and throws away. I have already had a conference with the principal, and Jim's overseeing teacher, who is marvelous, it appears.

Jim has always been told, it is too bad his ears got "broken," that it wasn't his fault. But it has never been used, or allowed, as an excuse for getting out of anything, or doing what he isn't supposed to, or slacking off. Through no fault of his own, there are things he will not be able to do in this world, because he has hearing problems. His LD exacerbates this.

The rules in place now state that, without certain math courses, Jim cannot obtain a high school diploma that will allow him to go to college. I am already taking steps to override that. I also just received my certification to substitute teach in the system, to better keep an eye/grip on what is going on and being done. My philosophy has always been that, with me around, they will sometimes do right just to shut me up. The children and I are in ongoing counseling at a nearby university, to make sure that nothing is being missed or overlooked. Jim is declared a very bright, social, stable, and outgoing individual—much more so than most of his counterparts.

We are still in touch with the former deaf tutor, who has gone through much of the same thing. I attempt to help others who have to deal with these matters, but who don't know where or how to begin. Seeing as everyone seems to know who I am and that I can be counted on to put in my two cents worth, or listen, folks come to me who are having similar problems. I try to help them realize they DO have a say, that there ARE laws, and that you CAN be noisy without getting your child in trouble. Heck, they already ARE having trouble, and being quiet about it won't fix it, by and large.

It has been a continual fight, from almost kindergarten on, to get those in charge to do just the basics that are needed. Those who are caring and want to really help, or even just do their jobs, seem few and far between. A parent who is involved and tries to be on top of things is often resented, rather than appreciated. In Jim's case, the paperwork, letters, etcetera, take up close to a full banker's box. Too many days started with the constant nagging, "What will go wrong or happen today?"

If this happens in a home where there is a parent who learned not to care what was said about her so long as they did right by her children, what is happening to the children who have no parent or person who gives a darn, or just allows it all to fall through the cracks?

Activities

1. Devise a system for monitoring Jim's IEP and sharing it with Bright Star to assure her that Jim is receiving the proper services.

2. Make two lists: (a) list everything that Bright Star looks for in a teacher and (b) list the teacher behaviors that are bothersome to Bright Star.

3. Conduct research on Apache or other tribal customs and cultural perspectives, particularly regarding disability and children.

4. *Discuss:* If Bright Star were asked to summarize the most important things that new teachers should understand about collaborating with families, what would she say?

5. *Discuss:* If you were Jim's special education teacher, how would you handle the situation with Jim's computer teacher who thinks Jim asks too many questions and who threw away Bright Star's letter? What should the principal do, if anything, now that the principal has had a meeting with Bright Star?

6. Role-play a conference between the special education teacher, the principal, and Bright Star in the situation that was presented in activity 5.

7. Using the information presented about Jim's skills and school behaviors, write a narrative progress report addressing the areas of reading and citizenship and work behaviors. Use the academic information you can glean from Bright Star's story and invent the additional details needed to be appropriately specific.

8. *Discuss:* How could a teacher of students with mild or moderate disabilities assure Bright Star that they had sufficient knowledge about hearing impairments to teach Jim effectively?

9. *Discuss:* Suggest the ways that teachers or administrators could use Bright Star's knowledge and energy advantageously.

10. Conduct an Internet search to locate a local support group for adoptive parents. Ask an adoptive parent to speak to your class about the unique situations or challenges that arise around school issues.

11. From Bright Star's descriptions, list the accommodations that you think might be helpful to Jim in his regular classes. Using the IEP format utilized in your local school district, determine how these accommodations could be written into the IEP.

12. It is important to Bright Star that teachers are willing to listen to what she knows about Jim's disabilities and how he learns. Develop a list of what you could learn

from Bright Star. Write a note to Bright Star that demonstrates your willingness and desire to learn from her.

13. Invite a school district mediator to speak to your class about dispute resolution and effective mediation strategies.

14. The various terms used to label hearing impairments can be confusing to both parents and professionals, especially because the terms go in and out of favor over time. Can you differentiate *deafness, hard of hearing,* and *hearing impairment?*

15. Do you understand Bright Star's distrust of school testing? Name two events or facts that might have contributed to this distrust.

16. Describe the best practices that teachers and other helping professionals should use to assist this family.

17. Write an analysis of this case, drawing parallels from this case to (a) your own experiences; (b) theory and research from class discussions, course readings, and knowledge gained in previous classes; and (c) other cases in this book.

Suggested Resources

American Speech-Language-Hearing Association. (2000, April 20). *Questions and answers about otitis media, hearing and language development.* Available for download at www.kidsource.com/ASHA/otitis.html

Beach Center on Disability (2000). *How to deliver services to Native American families who have children with disabilities.* Lawrence, KS: University of Kansas. Available for download at www.beachcenter.org

DiTomasso, L. (2002, January/February). A memo to my fellow teachers [Electronic version]. *Adoptive Families Magazine, 22.*

McPherson, C. F., & Minton, J. M. (1994). *Our Native American child: A guide for those who adopt and their supporters.* Southfield, MI: Spaulding for Children.

Stroud, J. E., Stroud, J. C., & Staley, L. M. (1999). *Adopted children in the early childhood classroom. ERIC Digest.* Champaign, IL: ERIC Clearinghouse on Elementary and Early Childhood Education. (ERIC Document Reproduction Service No. ED426819)

Online Resources

Visit the Web site of the National Indian Child Welfare Association [NICWA] at www.nicwa.org for information on the Indian Child Welfare Act of 1978.

References

Indian Child Welfare Act of 1978, Pub. L. No. 95-608, USC Title 25, Chapter 21, §1915.

CHAPTER FIVE

To Break the Chain: Aunt Rhonda's Story

Commentary: Rhonda is a 37-year-old White woman who grew up in a rural area in extreme poverty and who now lives in a large metropolitan area. Her niece and nephew live with their father in his mother's home. The children's mother and father are divorced and they both are heavily involved with drugs. Rhonda's 8-year-old nephew, Billy, is a child with attention deficit hyperactivity disorder (ADHD). Although Rhonda has to contend with her own emotional problems, she has been the one consistent adult on which these children could depend. Her story demonstrates how personal and family problems can overshadow a parent's concern with educational matters, requiring educators to develop interdisciplinary approaches to support their students' needs. This story provides a glimpse into one family member's attempt to break the cycle of several generations of abuse and neglect. In addition, it provides teachers with an opportunity to address how a family system's approach could enable teachers to support what Aunt Rhonda is attempting to teach her nephew, Billy.

TOUGH SINCE BIRTH

Billy is, hopefully, the last link in a chain of dysfunction that makes up my family. He is the son of two alcohol- and substance-abusing parents, grandson to an emotionally distant grandmother, and nephew to me, a survivor of these same emotional traumas. With psychological and spiritual counseling and drug therapy, not only did I survive, but at last I am truly beginning to live, to grow, to be. Those kids, Billy and his sister, Carol, are really what made me go and seek professional help. That's how important these kids are to me. The one time that I was really going to kill myself, I had just gotten beyond all hope. I looked at their picture, and I realized I couldn't leave. They had to have somebody. I'm not setting myself up like the great white hope, but their mom had left them and their dad was sliding back down into drugs again. They needed me.

These have been tough times for Billy. Billy is now 8 years old. He is a dark-haired boy with stormy blue eyes that seem to reflect what is going on inside of him. From the time he was born, he was a hyper child with an attention span that was either focused exclusively on one subject or would jump like lightning from one activity to another. As a baby, Billy did not like to be rocked or cuddled gently. He wanted to be held and walked around the room, or go riding in the car. He always wanted to be on the move. Gently rocking in a chair or just being cuddled close was almost impossible to do with Billy. If you wanted a hug, he would stiffen up and lean up against you. In some ways I thought he was autistic, but he communicated so well. He would be playing a game and be losing and he'd swish the whole game. He talked in his sleep a whole lot. Just constantly on the move, and when he wanted information about stuff there was no waiting, it had to be right then and now, this second. If his demands were not met immediately, all hell would break loose. Daily life was just a constant battle, trying to keep up with him. You had to keep an eye on him at all times.

BILLY OFF RITALIN

Billy has been on Ritalin for the last 2 years. The difference between Billy on and off Ritalin is amazing. You would almost think he is two different boys. During the summer months when he's not in school, Billy does not take Ritalin. These are very hard times for all of us. I love that kid, but let me give you a dose of what it's like to be with Billy. Last summer, I took the kids on vacation to Arkansas to my mom's house. It was the classic vacation from hell. Nine days before our scheduled departure date, I suffered a light stroke. Since lies and broken promises from their parents were a constant fact for Billy and Carol, I went against medical advice and my own good common sense, and left in an unairconditoned car with a 5 and 6 year old. It was foolish, but I swore I would not break my promise to these kids. The doctor told me to at least not drive over a couple of hours at a time.

I tried to get the car fixed before we left. I had planned to leave at 8:00 a.m, but we got to the service station at about 9:00 a.m. About 12:00 p.m. the guy finally says he doesn't know how to fix it, and this is deep into summer and it is hot. By this time, I'm upset and Billy is upset because he's been waiting so long. When he is upset, he is even more hyper.

He wanted a Coke, so we get a Coke. He took a few sips. He wanted pretzels and took a couple of bites and didn't want those. He would want something else. We didn't get 20 miles down the road until Billy had to go to the bathroom. Now we had just left a service station, but Billy has this fascination with bathrooms. I guess most kids are like that. Maybe he wants to be a bathroom architect, and this is just practical experience for him and he's looking for a variety of ideas. Anyway, we pull off and stop at the bathroom. I'm trying to keep my cool. We'll get down the road a little more and it'll be OK. It better be OK because this is the first vacation I've had in 3 years, and I'm going to enjoy it. I don't care if it kills me. I'm going to enjoy it, and so is Billy.

Billy was in the front seat. He started kicking the dashboard, and I'm yelling "Stop it!" and shaking his poor little old arm while screaming at him. I drive a few more miles and there is a sign that says "Motel—free breakfast—$24.95." I don't care if we've only driven an hour and a half, I put the brakes on and we're stopping. We're on vacation, and we're stopping, and we're here to enjoy it. I have cooled off, so I apologize to Billy and tell him that we are going to start our vacation now because we're going to have fun. By this time, I am totally wiped out. We haven't been gone 2 hours and I am completely exhausted. This shot my plans of getting at least halfway there in 1 day. We got 80 miles away from the city that day. I had to lay down, no way out of it. Finally, I get them calmed down. We're going to take a nap and then go swimming. Billy wants to know why, and I tell him

> Do you think that families with hyperactive children take fewer vacations?

because Aunt Rhonda said so. I tell him that I am tired and don't feel good. I hadn't told him about the stroke or anything like that. I just told him that I had gotten too hot one day and just didn't feel real good.

I got them to lay down and half an hour later we hit the swimming pool. He's going to have some fun. We're all going to calm down and cool off. Let him be a little boy. He runs right over and jumps right in the pool, and the child cannot swim. I run over and jump in after him and pull him out. He is screaming bloody murder. He doesn't like this place. He wants to go home. I tell him, "Hell, no, we're not going to go home. We're on vacation. We're going to have fun." Of course, by now there is a definite hysterical tone in my voice. Yes, we are going to enjoy this. With his attention span of a few minutes, he is back in the water. I tell him not to jump in the water or dunk his sister. She can't swim. I tell Billy not to play with the ball that belongs to the other little boy. We swim for about an hour and I try to get him out of the pool. He doesn't want to get out. He says he can swim by himself. I take him over and show him the pool sign— no children allowed by themselves. It's a pool rule. Billy doesn't like the rule but I explain that this is a rule that we're going to have to live by.

> Aunt Rhonda wants to educate and use reason with Billy and Carol. What guidelines could you provide to Rhonda about discipline that will be consistent with her desire to educate and to use reason with the children?

I get them back in the room and into the tub and washed off. It's the same thing. No water on the floor, no playing in the tub because that's the rules. Of course, there's water all over the floor and he's playing in the bathtub. He slips and hits the back of his head. It's another fit, crying and carrying-on and he wants to go home. He wants his Mickey. I go find his Mickey. He's had this Mickey ever since he was a very young child. A few minutes with Mickey and he forgot about it and is off on something else.

We are going to eat. I don't even want to think about eating. I just want to go to bed and sleep, and then start enjoying my vacation. Dinner is pretty much a repeat of the start of their day, and so is getting Billy to bed, and it's hard. After a shower and into his pajamas, we settle down for one story. It is his sister's turn to pick a story. She picks one out and that is not the one Billy wants to hear. He wheedles one more out of me.

> Aunt Rhonda does not live with Billy on a daily basis. How would this affect how she handles such situations? Would you provide different advice to Rhonda than you would to a daily caregiver?

The next day, Billy gets me up at 6:30 a.m. to go for a sunrise swim. The whole day starts. We get in our swimsuits and it is kind of a repeat of the day before. I constantly try to keep Billy from hurting himself or his sister and from driving me crazy. We take it pretty easy that day. We get started out sometime midmorning and we start to decide where to find a place to eat. Billy wants McDonald's, his sister wants Hardee's and I want to go to Denny's. We wind up at Denny's and Billy is in a foul mood by them. He doesn't want eggs, or any kind of breakfast food. He wants a hamburger and I can't really remember what I did. I think I gave in and ordered him a hamburger. Even in a restaurant with Billy, it's hard to keep him in his chair at the table. "Don't bounce on the seat. Don't kick the table leg. Leave the silverware on the other table alone. No, you can't take the little jellies off the other table."

It's hard trying to satisfy him with what is on the menu because he wants to order food you know he won't eat. It's "Billy, you know you won't eat that." "Yes, it's my favorite."

Sure, he wants a western omelet with onion and red and green peppers. I know he won't eat that, but he has it in his head that he would. You know, financially I can't let go of $7 bucks on a omelet for a child who I know won't eat that. It's like just throwing the money away. It's not depriving him of something he really needs. It's just that I know he will simply take a couple of bites and "Oh, I forgot I don't like this." I finally just gave in and let him have a hamburger. I think I even let him have a malt. Why not? We're on vacation.

We finally get through and get on the road. It was pretty much a play-by-play repeat of the day before, in and out of the seat, back seat to front seat, then he would start kicking. "Billy, stop the kicking." "I'm bored." "Well, honey, get one of your games." "I don't like those games." We had gone to Wal-Mart and got the little games to keep him entertained. He had played with them a couple of hours the day before. Now he was bored with them. But you know, this is part of Billy. It is a constant thing to hold his attention for more than 5 minutes. On this day I think we traveled a whole 2 hours.

WORRIES

Billy has a very sensitive side, too. I think it was the next day in the car that we're driving along, and I notice Billy is being quiet. At first, I think maybe he's asleep, but his foot is tapping lightly. As we keep driving along I start getting kind of worried. I'm starting to tense up and the back of my neck is getting tight. Carol has gone to sleep, so I ask Billy what's wrong. "Are you sick?" "No, I'm OK." "Does your tummy hurt?" "No." "Did you poo-poo this morning?" thinking he is constipated. I spent the next 10 miles going through everything I can think of that might be wrong. Finally, I just pull over and turn around. "Billy, what's wrong?" He looks at me with those big ole blue eyes and says "Aunt Rhonda, Arkansas's got so many dead people." It suddenly hit me, we've been driving the back roads and every little town has their cemetery just off the road. It's late summer, and in the small southern hill towns, it's a yearly custom to decorate the graves. So all of these cemeteries we've been passing have had fresh flowers on the graves. As far as he can see, people seem to be dropping like flies all over the place here. So we stop off at the next little place we come to and get out and walk around. We saw how old some of these dates were. We found some like from the 1800s. So that worry gets answered. All of a sudden, it's "Billy, get off the angel. No, Billy, don't run over the graves." He's back, folks. My boy's back.

So we get in the car and head back down the road and the questions begin. "Why do people die? What happens when people die? What is dying?" If going to heaven was so good, why did people cry? "Why do you put them in boxes? Why do you put them in the ground? Why is it people wear black?" He noticed that men are the ones who carry the caskets and he wants to know if girls carry the caskets for girls. Billy is so bright that he can come up with some really tough questions to answer. Just one question after another.

FEAR WILL MAKE ANYBODY QUIET

We finally arrive at Grammy's that day. It has taken me 3 days to drive what was a 7-hour trip. By the time we get there, I am exhausted. Now if I don't want to put up with two children, I damn well don't want to put up with my mom, who also can act like a child. She is really in some ways emotionally crippled. My mom can take the kids as long as she's not

> Do you find Aunt Rhonda's language offensive? If so, how would you deal with this type of language in a face-to-face meeting?

tired, or as long as they're not acting up, maybe a couple of hours together. It is so funny hearing her talk about "we" took care of the kids, or we took care of the luggage. It was always this "we" s***. Mom was just there. I had to load the car, and the kids slept in my room, and I stopped and found games. As long as all the conditions are right, she likes to be around them—going through her jewelry box, going for pizza, and watching a movie. But when they get whiney or cry, or when it comes to baths, food, anything to do with maintenance, that's when Mom disappears and Aunt Rhonda takes over.

This was just like when I was growing up. I was in the second, third, and fourth grades when the three babies were born. I'm out there changing their diapers, burping them, and walking them. I was out there scrubbing a whole washtub full of damned dirty diapers every Saturday. After I had gotten them scrubbed out, she handled the washing machine work and then I got to go hang them up. The really dirty stuff she didn't help, but you know she didn't see that.

Mom is clinically depressed, but you can't get her to admit to it. She thinks I'm the only nut out of the whole family because I'm the only one that's ever had therapy. She is always putting me down, and she acts like all the others are perfect. I finally told her, "I'm the most normal one you've got." I mean the whole family sucks, but I'm the only one who admits it. I got mad at Momma one day and I sat down and said, "Yeah, sure, you got six perfect kids. All your daughters are drunks or drug addicts. All of them have been prostitutes except for one and she's a hypochondriac. You've got one son that's a drunk, one that's a pervert, and one is a compulsive gambler. Yeah, Mom, you've got good kids."

She makes me so mad. Billy will have an accident and wet the bed. She would rather scold him and threaten to put a diaper on him, as opposed to getting him up in the middle of the night and make him go pee. She'll b**** about something or put you down, as opposed to trying to fix it.

After a couple of hours, Billy's having to hear from her how it is time for him to be a good boy and good boys are always quiet. If not, she wants to get into the spankings. That is not happening to my babies. "You're not beating on him like you beat on me." So now it is another strain to keep this extremely active child quiet long enough to keep his grandma from killing him or, if not killing him, beating him. She shouts at him, "Shut up!" She thinks if he wanted to be good, he could. "No, Mom, he's hyper and you screaming at him only upsets him and accelerates the problem." "Yeah, that's what's wrong with you damn kids these days. You just give over into your kids. Now when I was raising you kids, you kids knew better." I'm not brave enough to confront her yet, and tell her she beat the hell out of us. Fear will make anybody quiet, but it stifles and stunts. You're just not the person you could have been. They know that the children are not going to be subject to this kind of treatment. Not while I am around. It's a constant battle with my family not to fall into this.

SOMETIMES I'VE HAD IT

It's really hard to keep control sometimes though. I had to share a couch bed with the kids. The first night, Billy wants to go to a motel, and he argues about that for awhile. We finally get the couch folded out and I go to the bathroom. I stop to take a shower and I hear a scream.

> With the information that you know now about Billy's life, how would it affect the way you interact with him at school?

I rush back in there and Billy had jumped on the bed and hurt his foot on a metal crossbar. Now he's mad and I am frazzled. By this time I am wanting to pop his butt good, but think this is part of the dysfunction. If kids are loud, if they are obnoxious, if they are noisy, hit them 'til they cry and then they will be quiet. I barely make it this time. Finally we lay down crossways and they go to sleep and it is quiet.

Sometimes I can't handle it and I blow. The drive home did it to me. Billy's kicking seats, and he doesn't like this seat, he wants to switch with Carol. On and on and on. Finally, we stop and he switches. We go 10 or 15 miles and he says he wants his old seat back. I'm tired and frazzled, so I say OK. His sister doesn't want to switch. "OK, Billy, you wanted in that seat and you switched with your sister so now you're stuck with it." And then it's hollering and crying and "I hate you. You're mean to me. You don't love me no more."

It's just this constant thing. We stop off to eat a good lunch, and before we even get inside he says he doesn't like anything in there. He doesn't want chicken. He wants a hamburger. You know I've had it by this time. I pop him twice on the butt and feel guilty as hell after I do. I think, damn, you act just like your mother. You know, where is the therapy? Where is the coping skills? But, I swear, where is his control? I'm angry and upset with myself. I'm angry and upset with him. I'm angry and upset with the situation. I let him push me to this. I say to him, "Young man, you are going to go in there and sit down and you are going to be quiet. I'm going to go fix your plate and you are going to eat everything on it, and so help me if you don't I am going to bust your butt all the way back to the car." This works for awhile. I calm down, go in and sit down and I apologize. "Billy, I lost my temper. I did a bad thing. Just because you did a bad thing doesn't mean that Aunt Rhonda should do a bad thing."

After we get back in the car, it's another hellish 4 hours before we got home. He was so cranked up, so wired up, so exhausted, just literally moving his little body around, kicking his legs, in and out of the seat, wanting to go over the seat. He wants this game. He wants that game. He wants to color. He wants to read. He wants to play cards. He wants to play I Spy. He wants the radio on. He wants the radio off. It's just one want after another. That's Billy on vacation from Ritalin.

THE BREAK UP OF A FAMILY

His short little life has been mostly hard. My brother-in-law, Johnny, was in the service, and both kids were born in Germany. After they all got back from Germany they lived here 6 months, and then Johnny got sent to Saudi. He was only back about 2 months and he was sent to Korea for a full year. They had a happy secure environment, though. Their mom was always there, and for awhile there she was a good mother. They were used to their father going in and out of their lives because he was a soldier. That's what Daddy does, he goes to wars.

After they moved back from Germany, my mom and me were seeing the kids absolutely every weekend. Lydia would come and drop them off every Friday as soon as Billy got out of kindergarten, and we wouldn't see her until Sunday afternoon. Sometimes during the summer she would leave them here for a whole week at a time. By the time Johnny got back from Korea, my sister had gotten back into drugs again. They were sort of recreational users before, but when he was gone she really got into it. She dropped about 40 or 50 pounds.

Three days after Johnny got back, she's gone. They went to a party, and she left and went to live with her lover who was a drug dealer. She just left the kids with Johnny, abandoned them. When he filed for divorce, she didn't even bother to show up to get custody or anything. Billy was just 5 years old and Carol was 4.

Johnny and Lydia fought back-and-forth for a month or two. Billy wanted to know why grown-ups beat on each other. Lydia took a hammer after Johnny one day, right there in front of the kids. The kids have seen Johnny more than once go jerk her out of the house, beat the s*** out of her, and then drive off. Once she called the police, and Johnny spent a couple of days in jail. When he got out, he was angry at her, and he didn't want her to see the kids. He really used the kids big time to try to rope her into coming back to him.

> The American Psychologi-cal Association (1996) esti-mates that over 3 million children witness family vio-lence each year.

He wasn't letting Mom and me see the kids either. I didn't see the kids for a month, which almost drove me to breakdown. The whole damn thing was a nightmare. This was when I was going through my own nervous breakdown type thing. I've been haunted by nightmares for years. I woke up scared s***less, soaked in sweat, my heart's pounding, and I could not remember a thing. Then, when I started remembering, it was horrid. I isolated in the room. I remember I had put Reynolds Wrap over the window to have absolutely no contact with the outside world. The kids were my joy. They were the best thing in my life. I had never experienced unconditional love like I felt with them. I had been pregnant three times, and all three times I lost my babies. You think you can love something, but it's not until you experience it that you realize the extent of it. It's really hard to describe.

I threatened to take Johnny to court. I had really got tired of being jerked around. The kids were suppose to come over and come spend the weekend with me. Johnny said Lydia had broke some promise to him. That's when I'd had enough. I just told him that I would take him to court because grandparents and aunts do have rights now. I was pretty upset, probably more or less screaming at him. And I told him to stop punishing me. I said, "Johnny, you know those kids love me. You're hurting them too." And he was! I think Johnny really knew I was very serious about this.

The first time I saw the kids after that was when he had to go out on the boat for 48 hr. I guess the kids had to be dying before he could leave his post, so this was something he had to do. He made me promise that if Lydia showed up, I was to lock the door, and call the police. She was not to see them. Fine, I agreed to that. He was their father and that was his decision to make. All I cared about was me getting to see them, and I wasn't going to risk that.

Lydia was off doing her own thing anyway. She was really bad. Now prior to that I thought maybe she was tuttin' some coke or something like that, but I didn't realize the extent. Now that she was living with a drug dealer, she was bumping probably four or five times a day. I think she felt kind of guilty 'cause she didn't want to see them, and she'd make a bunch of promises she wasn't going to keep. She was supposed to come over and see him one time. "Yes, son, I'm going to come over and we're going to spend some time. We're going to go get pizza." She never showed up. She never called. Billy got so angry, he just demolished this huge plant I had. It was lush and beautiful, and the vines on it were at least 4 to 5 feet long. I don't have that many nice things, and I came unglued and spanked his hands. I felt so bad for hitting him. You know, the kid comes from this. That doesn't excuse what he did, but we're trying to get him to a different manner to express his anger.

I remember another night, Johnny brought the kids over to the house and she came over to see them. Her and Billy were going to walk to the store. They had walked part of the way down the street and this little dog ran out. Billy was terrified of dogs, and he got hysterical and was trying to climb up on her. She was screaming and hollering at him and dragging him back instead of just picking him up. I was so angry. I could see she was out of control, and she was hurting him. She needed a fix, or she had too much, or I don't know what her problem was. When he seen me, he come running toward me, he was just so terrified. That is one of the few times I had struck her. I didn't blame Johnny for not wanting her around the kids. Me and Momma was scared that she would take the kids and run with them. And she was the last person we wanted to have the kids.

Over the next 6 months, Johnny and Lydia made two or three attempts of getting back together. They started doing drugs together again. Johnny had always smoked a little weed and drank. He had really started getting into drugs toward the last few months he was in the army. I guess he figured, "Well, she's back in it, so why can't I?" But he was still not like she was. She'd be there a few days and then right back to a user, dealer, lover, whatever. Him and her were periodically fighting. It was mostly verbal. She would make him mad, and he would tell the kids "Your momma's a g*ddamn speed-whore, slut. Suck anything she can get her hands on for a shot." This was all true, but the kids did not need to hear this all the time. Billy asked me one time what "speed-whore" was. He says, "Daddy calls that to Momma all the time." And he said, "I know what a pimp is." I'm not denying anything Johnny said, and I'm not denying that she called him names too. I totally agree that they're both jerks. I threatened to call Child Protective Service if they didn't stop this name calling in front of the kids every time they run into each other. They could go off and kill themselves for all I cared. They was just doing so much damage to the kids, to listen to this s***.

> If this language makes you cringe, imagine what it does to a child! But examine it again. What is most damaging to the children—the particular words, the message about their mother's character, or the expressed hostility? Would an intervention with Johnny need to address all three issues?

You could really see some big changes coming over the kids. Before that, they were so carefree and happy and secure. Billy's behavior really started getting extreme, which we put down to the divorce. His medical condition just intensified it.

GROWN-UP PROBLEMS

Billy's very confused, and he feels very guilty. Bad enough their mother deserted them, but their dad was telling them, "She don't love you. She wouldn't have walked off and left you if she loved you." My mom was always telling him he was a bad boy whenever he did anything wrong. So he thought it was his fault she left because he was such a bad boy. I explained to him, "No, Billy, your mother had other reasons to leave and they were having nothing to do with you." "Well, Granny says I am bad. Momma used to scream at me all the time. She said I was driving her crazy." I said, "Billy, sometimes adults can be very

Can teachers approach parents' problems as openly as this with children? What would you say?

ugly. Just because you are an adult does not mean you're right, or that you do the right thing. That's why you need to learn and pay attention to what's right and what's wrong."

I don't want him to see them and think when he grows up he can act like that and it's OK. It's not ever OK. He wants to know if she loves him, if she's coming back, and what's wrong with her. "Billy, your momma's got problems and they are grown-up problems. They are just too big for kids to carry around. When you see your mom, love her. Enjoy her and the time you spend with her. Just realize that she's got big problems, and she can't work them out when she's at home. She had to leave to work them out."

Johnny moved up here with the kids so his mom could look after the kids. He's got free room and board over there. Johnny can't make it out of an environment like the army. That's the way Johnny was raised, and the army has a certain thing to do at a certain time. After Lydia left, he really went down. Lydia was kind of the glue that kept everything together. And when that was gone, the army didn't mean all that much. Then he got back into the drugs, and he knew it was either get out or get discharged. He's been job-to-job. Since he spent so many years in the army, he would be real high up. But he's already been out twice, and they won't take him in a third time. He's been to the National Guard, and goes and trains once a month for a weekend. If a war broke out, they'd take him back in a heartbeat; but during peace, he's just dead weight.

I see why Johnny's the way he is. If Johnny does good, he's well loved. If he's not doing good, he ain't s*** to his mom. Her husband come from poor white trash, and he done real good. She's always tried to act the genteel thing that just don't quite wash. His mother's got blinders on. All she does is see what she wants to see. Her home is real cold and immaculate. Glass shines everywhere; the windows never get dirty.

The kids sleep upstairs with their father in the attic where he slept as a kid. They have a playroom with every game, every video, every toy, a little vanity, and a little desk. This is where children are put, and this is where they stay. They're trotted out for guests when they're all cleaned up. Otherwise they're shoved back there in the bedroom. They're not allowed outside in the yard to play because the neighborhood is bad. She walked in her house once and a guy that was breaking in was still in her house. She screamed and the mailman comes flying through the door and saved her ass. I agree with her not letting the kids out of the yard unsupervised. I know how many weirdos and sickos there are out there. I know they go anywhere and everywhere. But it's really sad. She's kind of a cold person, and if the kids do good in school they're given a dollar, maybe a few minutes of her time. You can tell they're just starved for adult attention. Every time I go over there they're back in the bedroom. They're real distant from her. They don't even call her Grandma.

THE TEACHER STARTED THE BALL ROLLING

Billy had just graduated kindergarten when they moved in with Johnny's mom. I remember he had his little graduation picture with his little white graduation uniform. They were so cute. He just barely passed first grade. That was when they put him on Ritalin, but it was a real low dose. I really think it was the teacher that started the ball rolling. She just probably couldn't deal with him. I know Child Protective had been called in. Johnny had to deal with it then. He didn't tell me anything and the teacher didn't tell me anything, and they're not the kind of people that'll really try to butt in. But the best I can figure out, it was probably Billy's teacher that realized there were some problems there. Billy said that there were lots of meetings, and that somebody came to talk to the kids. Johnny went to some counseling sessions, but it was more that he had to because Child Protective had been in on it. Johnny always put Billy's behavior down as being a brat or just being a boy. I think that it was really hard for him to accept the fact that his son needed medication or that he had any mental problems.

When Billy went into school this year, it took his dad almost 2 months before we could get him to go up and get him a prescription. It finally came down to the school telling him that he needed to get this done or they would call the child protection agency. I talked to his teacher, and it was the same behavior at school. Billy would go around and pick on kids and pull out chairs and swipe things. He would get so frustrated when he worked that he would tear the work up and break colors. He would get to coloring so hard that he would break crayons. His average scores were in the 50s and 60s. He was failing second grade big time. The teacher was at her wit's end. Not only did she have Billy, she had 20 other children to keep up with and educate.

After Johnny got his medication, within 2 weeks Billy won Citizen of the Week award. By the end of the year, his lowest grade was a 97. His citizenship went from unsatisfactory to excellent. He had lots of *E*s with time management, finishing assignments, social skills, completing assignments, listening attentively, and using his time wisely. It has just made an amazing difference to him. I just can't image him not on Ritalin and going to school. You can't just keep a kid doped up all the time, but there is certainly an appropriate time and place. While he is in school, he needs to be on Ritalin. It does not slow his mental capacity. He has attention deficit disorder. It's like putting a 33 record on 78. His mind goes so fast he can't concentrate. It makes him nervous and irritable to be like that. What Ritalin does is it slows him down. He's not in a stupor or a zombie. I guess with abuse and misuse it could make kids like that. He's just calmer. But he made such perfect grades the last time. He brought his average back up to 90 and it had been like 70. So you know the Ritalin just made almost a miraculous difference in his behavior.

> What do you suppose Billy's teachers really know about his life? Do you imagine that Carol's teacher sees any fallout from her family life?

Carol was in first grade this year and her average score is 92. Both their scores are so good that they both won scholarships to a private year-round school. Billy said he didn't know that smart kids were punished and they had to go to school all year. That's what he's feeling like. I'm so excited for the both of them. Carol's excited. She just loves school. She loves to learn. Billy likes to go through the highlights of it. Getting down into the details and stuff, he don't like. But he's becoming more and more aware that he needs to slow down and absorb more. They're so different, yet they're so alike in some ways. And they have a good relationship together. They fight and squabble. But I think through all this crap, that they're even more bonded than most brothers and sisters are because all they have is each other. For one thing they're so close in age. I've kind of noticed, Carol is being groomed to be the caretaker. When they're with me, they pick up their own toys. I don't take responsibility for their clothes or their shoes. Carol would jump in. I need to talk to Johnny about this. Carol does not need to be her brother's fixer. Billy needs to settle down and start fixing things on his own.

LACK OF OPTIONS

At this time, Lydia and Johnny have kind of resolved they were not getting back together, and it's gonna be beneficial for them to kind of work it out. They had kind of got to where they were being very civil to each other, after maybe a year and a half. I really notice that he doesn't put her down in front of the kids, and Lydia doesn't either. On occasion, when she's between boyfriends and he's between girlfriends, they get together. Deep down they do still really care for each other. I think it's so tragic that they can't get past these damned drugs and get back together and make it again. He says he doesn't want her. She says she doesn't want him. But if he goes to jail, she's bailing him out. He broke into a motel room where she was with her dealer. He beat the s*** out of him and knocked her around. They took him to jail, and she raised bail to get him out of jail! Whenever she got popped, he was trying to raise some bail to get her out of jail. If she's with somebody that beats her up or rips her off or whatever, Johnny will go get her.

Billy just seems more accepting of Mom and Dad's strange behavior. Kids pick up what their boundaries are, what they can do. When he's with his mother, he is whiney and demanding and just a brat. And this is the way his mother deals with it. And that's the way he deals with his mother. What I'm trying to do is make him aware, "Look, Billy, I know you act this way with your mother, but I'm not accepting it. You don't act that way with me." I try to reinforce "You're a good, smart boy. And you know what needs to be done."

I think if I was in the position to offer the kids a home, Johnny would let me have them. He's so far down into the drug scene. In the last few months he's lost 60 pounds. He's really tried to go and straighten it out a few times, but it just didn't last long. I had the kids at a friend's house all last week, and he was really eager to get rid of the kids for a week. He loves the kids, though, and he was glad to see them when I brought them back home. His mom is refusing to take any responsibility for keeping the kids. Lydia wouldn't want them either. She might say she would. Something would come up and she couldn't, but there's no way she could deal with them. Lydia's too strung out to be the mother she was. I know that a lot of times she really puts that effort out. But she's all cranked up on the amphetamines, and for one thing she can't sit still long enough. And then they get on her nerves. She's already strung, so they make it worse. Both of them, but Carol is a lot calmer than her brother. You can give her some colors and paper and especially a good book with pictures and she can entertain herself for a long, long time.

Johnny's a good dad through the most of it. Outside of this thing with Lydia, he's still affectionate, still loving. He's nurturing, as much as a trained killer can be. Johnny's very seriously army. Johnny could strip a machine gun in 30 seconds. That's why he's not doing worth a s*** out here now. It really surprises me how it turned out. But he was a good dad. He learned how to comb little 4-year-old girl's hair and put it up. And then seeing him try to button little tiny buttons, and color-coordinate socks and shirts together. He helps Carol dress her Barbie dolls and has tea parties with her. Billy and Johnny are boys together.

I'm not getting to see the kids near as much as I want to because of where I'm living. It's a women's mission with strict rules, and kids aren't allowed. I go by, and we go out to McDonald's, or we go to a park. During this deep summer I don't see them as much. I got Carol in the Girl Scouts and they didn't take her over there to them. The way my work schedule was, I couldn't. They've got Vacation Bible School all over the place around here, but you know their grandmother. I don't blame her; these are not her children. She's already raised her kids. Johnny won't get them ready; he's not too crazy about religion anyway.

It's tough for Johnny because he's used to leaving them with me every weekend. So now he's just kind of leaving them with anybody he can. Johnny left the kids with my older sister and her husband for a weekend and I blew. My brother-in-law is not anybody I would leave the kids alone with. Billy is so hyper, it's like leaving a cap and a stick of dynamite together. My sister called me up and was telling me about it, and I went and got the kids. I just told Johnny don't leave them. Johnny knows I've got him by the balls, because he knows I know that he's on drugs. Johnny really knows that when it comes down to the kids, I would snitch on him. That makes a difference to him. I think he thought it would be really perfect if I had the kids and then he could see them when he was ready to. But he would not want them legally taken away where he didn't have control or access. He loves the kids. Lydia loves the kids. They're just both messed up on dope. That's what is so tragic…because of the potential that's there. Why can't they straighten themselves out?

Activities

1. As Billy's teacher, write a letter to his father to explain Billy's behavioral problems in class and to ask him to call you to discuss what to do.

2. Prepare a packet of readings on managing the behavior of children with ADHD geared to Aunt Rhonda's needs.

3. Design a workshop for families to learn about attention deficit hyperactive disorder.

4. *Discuss:* How could you educate people about the negative consequences of labeling a child as a "bad boy," as did Billy's grandmother? What should you say or do if you hear another teacher reprimand a child by saying that the child is bad?

5. *Discuss:* If Rhonda gets so angry with her mother, why did she visit her mother for her vacation? Why do children who are abused still love, and sometimes protect, their parents?

6. It can be difficult to communicate with parents about problem areas when you are also concerned about low self-esteem or harsh discipline. Using the information about Billy's achievement and behavior, complete a progress report for Billy that describes both his achievements and his deficits. Devise whatever additional information you require to complete the progress report. To whom would you send this

report? Are you allowed to send the progress report to anyone else? Are you obligated to send the report to anyone else?

7. Could Aunt Rhonda be a volunteer in the classroom? List her strengths and the tasks that you would request of her. Outline the preparation you would provide to her before her first day as a volunteer.

8. Conduct research on the availability and quality of foster homes in your area. Invite a caseworker to the class, and interview the caseworker to determine the caseworker's viewpoint on the quality of placements. Provide the caseworker with a list of questions that you wish to discuss, which also should include the following questions: What is the average time that a child stays in foster care? What is the typical number of home placements for a child who is in the foster care system? What is the rate of abuse in foster care? How successful are these children as adults?

9. Search the professional literature for outcome data on children placed in foster care. What is the average time that a child stays in foster care? What is the typical number of home placements for a child who is in the foster care system? What is the rate of abuse in foster care? How successful are these children as adults?

10. *Discuss:* Would Billy and his sister, Carol, be better off if they no longer saw their mother? As a teacher, what are your legal obligations for reporting parental behavior? Would Billy and Carol be better off if they lived elsewhere? What are their options? Why are these options better or worse than their current situation? How might your opinions on these matters affect your behavior as a teacher?

11. What are this family's needs? What agencies should be involved, and what services does the family need? Conduct research to find the appropriate agency names, addresses, contact names, and telephone numbers for your local area.

12. We did not hear from Billy's father in this story—his perspective of the issues, what his needs were, and so forth. Pretend that you are Johnny, who is reading what Rhonda wrote, and write a one-page response explaining your perspective about what Rhonda says.

13. Aunt Rhonda indicates that Billy's father, Johnny, has not been responsive to teachers' requests. Can you think of unique strategies that might increase this father's presence at school or increase his involvement in Billy's educational process?

14. Assume that the court has ordered Billy's father, Johnny, to participate in counseling and parenting classes. Design a parent education program for Johnny. What topics would you choose, and what structure would you use? What are the variables and assumptions that influence your design process?

15. *Discuss:* How much of Billy's hyperactivity do you believe should be attributed to ADHD and how much should be attributed to his environment and learned behavior?

16. Describe the best practices that teachers and other helping professionals should use to assist this family.

17. Write an analysis of this case, drawing parallels from this case to (a) your own experiences; (b) theory and research from class discussions, course readings, and knowledge gained in previous classes; and (c) other cases in this book.

Suggested Resources

Edelson, J. L. (1999). Children's witnessing of adult domestic violence. *Journal of Interpersonal Violence, 14*(8), 839–870.

Forness, S. R., Sweeney, D. P., & Toy, K. (1996). Psychopharmacologic medication: What teachers need to know. *Beyond Behavior, 7*(2), 4–11.

Groves, B. M. (2002). *Children who see too much: Lessons from the child witness to violence project.* Boston: Beacon Press.

Kearney, M. (1999). The role of teachers in helping children of domestic violence. *Childhood Education, 75*(5), 290.

Knitzer, J. (2000). *Promoting resilience: Helping young children and parents affected by substance abuse, domestic violence, and depression in the context of welfare reform.* New York: National Center for Children in Poverty.

National Institutes of Health. (1998, November 16–18). Diagnosis and treatment of attention deficit hyperactivity disorder. *NIH Consensus Statement Online, 16*(2), 1–37. Available for download at odp.od.nih.gov consensus.nih.gov/cons/cons.htm#1998

Payne, R. K. (1998). *Framework for understanding poverty.* Highlands, TX: RFT Publishing Company.

Online Resources

Visit the Web site of Children and Adults with Attention Deficit Hyperactivity Disorder (CHADD) at www.chadd.org

References

American Psychological Association (1996). *Violence and the family: Report of the APA presidential task force on violence and the family.* Washington, DC: Author.

One Last Chance, Again: Frank's Story

Commentary: Contrary to a usual stereotype, single fathers, instead of mothers, may have custody of their children. Frank, a White father in his 50s, took custody of his adolescent son after his ex-wife apparently wore out or gave up. She was also worried for the safety of her new baby. For as long as Frank can remember, their son, Greg, has had severe behavioral problems. Greg is also a child with attention deficit hyperactivity disorder (ADHD). You will hear the frustration of a parent who has never known how to deal with his son, in spite of great love and consultation with numerous therapists. It appears that no one has ever known how to get through to Greg. Consequently, Greg has had little consistency as he tries therapist after therapist, challenges school after school, and wears out one parent or another.

Frank initially viewed the problems with Greg simplistically, attributing inadequate parenting on his ex-wife's part as a factor of Greg's behavior, until he met the same challenges. This case presents a major challenge to the reader to avoid simplistic judgments and answers, blaming one person or another for what they did or did not do, or to recommend obvious solutions that overlook the complexity or reality of this situation. In addition, this case provides an opportunity to examine your own family values; that is, your beliefs about what a family is, what the obligations of a family are, and what impact the break up of relationships have on a family. This case also provides an opportunity to discuss the ties between the juvenile justice system, the education system, and the mental health system. Can these systems meet the present-day needs for Frank and his ex-wife to find the appropriate services and support to deal with Greg's disturbing behaviors? The renewal of energy that is needed to ensure their younger son, Jeff, avoids the same problems is at stake. Depression and burnout are very real possibilities, which would have a negative impact on Jeff.

EVEN AS A BABY

Greg was a somewhat troubled child, even as a baby. He cried and fussed a great deal more than other babies, demanding attention on a continual basis. For example, at about 13 months, we found out that he was manipulating us. We had gone to his pediatrician anxious about his frequent crying. The doctor told us to put a tape recorder in his room to see exactly what was going on. We did, the result being that Greg would scream his lungs out for several minutes at a time, then become quiet, clearly playing with crib toys, then go back to screaming. It was an eye-opener.

Greg was 3 years old, and his brother about 4 months, when we separated. I would pick up the boys on Friday nights for the weekend. Once, when we were heading home from Burger King, Greg's favorite place to eat, he turned to me while I was driving and asked if I had left because he was a bad boy. It sent me into tears. I told him that no, sometimes people just couldn't get along with each other, and that was what had happened between his mother and I. I also told him that if I had left because he was bad, I wouldn't be spending time with him on the weekends. That seemed to satisfy him. This "bad boy" thing was a recurring theme with my ex-wife, though, and as early as 6 or 7 years old, he would refer to himself as a "bad boy." She would repeatedly tell the kid that he was "bad," basically reinforcing an already low opinion of himself.

> According to Sprague and Walker (2000), mounting evidence suggests that antisocial behavior patterns are preventable if problems are identified and treated upon school entry.

As he grew older, Greg became far more demanding of attention, mostly negative. No amount of positive feedback to him about school, artwork, or other accomplishments had any effect on his behavior, which became worse as he got older. By worse, I mean that he became more violent in his approach to others. This was especially prevalent with his brother, Jeff. From the time Jeff was able to toddle, Greg would terrorize him in almost every imaginable way. For example, Jeff had a favorite toy, a stuffed animal. Greg tied a string around the neck of the toy and teased Jeff by pulling it along the floor, just out of his reach. Jeff was barely walking, frequently falling, and his attempts to reach the toy were clearly pitiful. Greg found great glee in tormenting him with it. He eventually destroyed the toy by tearing off its arms, legs, and head and giving it back to Jeff. To this day, Jeff fears Greg.

Greg's behaviors became dangerous to the household. He would light fires, acquire sharp objects such as knives or sharpened sticks, and create damage to the house itself, punching holes in walls. It was at this point, maybe 5 or 6 years old, that he was diagnosed as ADHD. A series of medications were tried, none of them seemed to work effectively, or for very long. Greg was always "prowling," mostly late at night when everyone else was asleep. He had no inner controls or restraints on his behavior, and his impulsivity caused him to get into more and more serious trouble. At the same time, he was utterly fearless and would take the most ridiculous dares from other children, often leading to injury to himself. He shrugged these off, saying that he was "tough." Fights at school became commonplace, with the other children becoming more frequently injured than Greg.

EXTENDED FAMILY

When Greg was 8 or 9, I became involved with a woman who had a 12-year-old daughter.

> What are your beliefs about couples living together outside marriage? How would your beliefs influence your communications with Frank and his partner?

We purchased a house together that was large enough for all three children to have their own rooms. As usual, during this period, Greg demanded and received the most attention, almost all of it negative. The boys would visit us on weekends and extended periods during school holidays. The three children got along well, for the most part. Greg still terrorized his brother, but got basically nowhere with my partner's daughter. They got along as most younger brothers and older sisters do—contempt tinged with love, or love tinged with contempt.

As an extended family, we did many activities together. My partner and I had a long-standing beach rental in Maine, and all of us went for at least 2 weeks every year. We set up rules and guidelines. For example, we frequently took all the kids out for dinner at various restaurants. The rule was act up during the meal, and one of the adults will take you out to the car and wait for the others to finish. By acting up, I don't mean the normal exuberance of a child out for dinner. I mean throwing food, fighting with the other kids, etcetera. In 99% of the cases, it was Greg who sat in the car with one or the other of us. I can't begin to count the number of dinners I've left sitting on the table. We were, of course, attempting to illustrate unacceptable behaviors. This approach had no effect whatsoever on Greg, nor do most punishments, as such. After awhile, we stopped going out to dinner.

Even though he was only with us for relatively short periods of time, Greg created a reputation among the kids in our neighborhood as someone to avoid. As an example, three siblings lived down the street. One of them was a school friend of my partner's daughter, so she was frequently at our house playing with Barbie dolls. One weekend when the boys were staying with us, the other children were all out in the driveway playing a game. Again, Greg chose to isolate himself. He had filled glass bottles with sand, making "bombs." Greg came out of the garage with his bombs and proceeded to throw them on the concrete, apparently enjoying the explosions. Jeff and my partner's daughter were already used to this kind of behavior, but this really frightened the three neighborhood children. They ran down the street, Greg chasing them, throwing more bombs. He didn't throw at them, but close enough to their feet that fright and alarm were generated. They never came back to play. This, of course, added to his growing isolation. No one would play with him. His mother relayed similar circumstances in her neighborhood. He once said to me, "If everyone already thinks I'm bad, then I might as well have fun at it." He was 9 years old when he told me this.

> If you were dealing with a parent who was experiencing such severe problems with a child's behavior at home, how would this influence the consequences that you, as the teacher, might elect to use? What types of consequences might have limited effectiveness? What school consequences might have a negative effect on the family?

For awhile at school, Greg was on the high end of the curve academically and the low end behaviorally. He was continually being suspended, serving detention, etcetera. He was tested as gifted and would score extremely high on tests and quizzes. But he failed subjects due to his inattention, disruptive behavior in class, and his refusal to do any homework. This pattern emerged early and remained with him throughout his schooling. I know that his mother had IEPs on Greg all along for his behavior problems, but nothing seemed to help.

It was about the time Greg was 10 that his mother moved away to Florida with the boys and her second husband. It was hard for me to determine the effect of this move on Greg. He and I had always been close, and I cried the day they left, in the boys' presence. He cried a bit as well, as did Jeff, but I feel that Greg accepted the separation as just another form of punishment for his being "bad." I have nothing concrete to validate this, it was just a feeling.

I did not see either of them for 2 years, but had frequent contact by phone and letter with both of them and their mother. She reported a serious escalation in Greg's behavior and that prescribed medication (Ritalin) was not working. Greg had started a fire in a corner of a school building and was expelled. His mother enrolled him in private school, and after less than a year, he was expelled from there as well. This last expulsion was from a series of incidents, mostly fights, all tinged with violence and impulsivity. She convinced the public school system to give him another chance, and his medication was changed.

GETTING REACQUAINTED

Ultimately, they made plans to move back up here, and I was called and asked if I would take the two boys for 6 weeks while the rest of the family moved. I agreed enthusiastically. It was an opportunity to become reacquainted after 2 years. I made plans for the vacation of a lifetime: a driving/exploration trip up the coast of Maine and on to Nova Scotia. It was, to say the least, a nightmare. The two of them fought incessantly, continually nit-picking about one thing or another. I had to keep them separated in the car, or I wouldn't have been able to drive. Their behaviors were embarrassing to me several times, as we stayed in hotels throughout our journey and, of course, ate in restaurants. Greg was, of course, the prime instigator of the problems. The difference was that Jeff was now older and more able to defend himself. This put Greg somewhat over the edge in terms of new terrorist routines. His favorite was to punch Jeff in the stomach when no one was looking, then turn around and say "Jeff, cut that out!" He became very adept at placing blame anywhere but on himself.

By this time, Greg had been "interviewed" by at least a half-dozen psychologists or psychiatrists, could formulate what they were going to ask or say, and develop "appropriate" responses. His mother and I frequently had to set them straight on several issues. He had them completely fooled. He would adopt the language that his mother and I, or teachers, would use in talking about his education and future, fully understanding it, as well as using it correctly in context. He would speak of "achieving goals" in his education, of his "plans for college," of his "process" for achieving the nonexistent goals. Some of these people came away from meetings with Greg with glowing terms about how mature and centered he was. It was a bit disturbing to me that they couldn't see through his facade. With others, he took an opposite approach, speaking of worshipping Satan and beating up everyone who yelled at him. There was always just enough child-speak mixed with the vocabulary of an adult. He was quite adept at the scam. He was then 12 years old.

The family settled into their new house, and I saw the boys quite frequently. Greg was now in junior high school and had started to attract the attention of the police. More and different medications were tried, all without success, as were various counselors. Greg's skill in defrauding counselors was now almost perfected. He had one poor, young intern at his school in tears, to his outright glee.

> Greg saw many therapists over the years, but Frank appears to believe they did little good. Can you speculate on the explanations that they might offer?

Their mother has relatives in England, and she had made plans to visit her grandmother, who was in poor health. She and I discussed the issue of whether or not to take Greg, because the rest of the family was all going. By this time, she had a young daughter by her second marriage. Greg was not allowed in the presence of the baby girl alone. He was deemed too dangerous. I convinced her to take Greg, as this was an opportunity for him to see another country. She reluctantly agreed.

About midway through the visit, I got a transatlantic call from her, telling me that Greg and her husband were on their way back. She was fed up. Either he would come to live with me, or he would go into foster care or a group home. He had apparently run roughshod through the relatives' household, then had run away to escape punishment. For her husband, it was the restaurant issue on a larger scale. He had to cut short his vacation because of Greg's behavior.

A FRESH START

I agreed to take Greg full-time, somewhat reluctantly because of the job I had at the time. But I did so because I felt that I could deal with him more effectively than his mother. To a degree it was my ego talking. On another level, it was the fact that I didn't want to see one of my kids in foster care, not without trying first. Greg was just barely 14 at this point.

In the beginning, I took a different approach. "There are just the two of us," I said, "and we both have to pitch in and do our parts. We are partners, you and I, and we have to get along together and make this work," etcetera, etcetera. Very pep-talky, I admit, but I felt very strongly that he needed a sense of belonging and no more isolation.

I was living in a small village in a small home. Both the boys had their own bedrooms, and Greg had a set of chores to do around the house. My job entailed a great deal of travel, and, due to his behavior history, I had to curtail that to the point of day trips only, no overnights. Even when I was gone during the day, I ensured that both Greg and his school had reliable contacts in case of problems. Because his mother had, for whatever reasons, basically dropped out of the picture, I had asked a good friend of mine to act in this role. She had a human services background and was happy to do it. Prior to settling upon her as an alternative to no travel, I had a great deal of difficulty with my job. Basically, I had to inform my management that because I was a single parent, I could not travel at all until I found an alternative. A great deal of pressure was put on me at this point, both at work and at home.

> Was Frank "wrong" in not sharing Greg's history with the school when Greg moved in with him? What motivated his decision? Would Greg's cumulative folder have told the school what they needed to know?

I was determined to give Greg a second chance and did not dwell upon his past problems when enrolling him in his new school. He was starting ninth grade in high school, in a completely new school, and I felt he needed a clean slate. I was wrong in this assessment.

The first manifestation of trouble came, surprisingly not from the school, but from the police. One evening, just after dinner, two state police officers came to the door and asked to talk to Greg and me. It seems that he was "prowling" again. After I had gone to sleep for the night, he was out wandering around the village stealing things out of cars. This is at 2:00 a.m. or 3:00 a.m. He was seen and tracked, as it was winter, and his tracks were clearly visible in the snow. I was, of course, appalled. In the first place, I had no idea this was going on. In the second, I felt betrayed by him. I had trusted him as a partner. He admitted everything. He even took the police to where he had hidden the things he had stolen. He didn't even want them, he said. And, looking at the items, I could see that they were trivial—a cigarette lighter, an audio tape, someone's driver's license, pens, a flashlight, etcetera. When asked why he did it, he replied, "I just wanted to." Out of Greg's hearing, I discussed with the police officers what was to be done. They said that they would not keep an official file, but that Greg should write apologies to each of the owners of the items, and deliver them personally. I asked the police to put him through the court system, to basically scare him. They refused. I often think of how he might have turned out if they had acquiesced.

After that, our relationship went downhill. There was no more pretense on his part about his opinion of me. He thought I was a fool. After all, he had gotten away with theft right under my nose. I, however, was not going to give up. Here was a kid who had an extremely low self-esteem, who considered himself "bad" beyond redemption. I wanted to help him find one thing that made him feel good about being Greg.

PARTNERING

His behavior at school, of course, became worse. I admitted to the school administration that I was less than forthcoming in terms of his past. Recriminations aside, we set up an Individual Education Plan for Greg with the special education department. I was fortunate enough to find that the special ed supervisor at his school was excellent at her job, which is not always the case. She was a true advocate for Greg. This began 4 years of one or sometimes two meetings weekly with the school.

The special ed supervisor and I organized the first IEP meeting with all concerned. It was interesting to note that the school administration chose not to attend any of these meetings. This changed when the supervisor and I went to the school board and insisted. This is not uncommon. I've found that school administrators frequently do not have much in the way of background in dealing with ADHD children, and have a habit of leaving all such interaction to the special education departments. To date, I have found this to be the case in three separate school systems. It is extremely disconcerting to attempt a holistic approach to an ADHD child's education, when several key players are unaware or lack knowledge of the issues and problems of such a child. This places an enormous burden on the special ed people and the parent.

For example, Greg and I lived in a rural area where school buses were the only mode of transportation. Due to an incident on the bus where Greg had started a fight, he was banned from riding the bus indefinitely. This was a standard, and typical, method of isolation by the school administration. Not knowing any better, I drove Greg to school every morning, arriving at work late every morning. Because of other incidents, Greg was not permitted to stay at school after normal class hours. I had to leave work early, every day, to pick him up and drive him home. This went on for about 3 months. Luckily, my management was understanding. It did, however, place a strain on my position. I finally asked the special ed supervisor if there was some option. She had been driving him home herself, out of her way, on days when I was just stuck for an option. Thus began a long, drawn-out series of meetings with the school administration, the bus supervisor, the school superintendent, and ultimately, the school board, to acquire school-paid transportation for Greg on a daily basis. In essence, there was no facility for these kids and no standard method of dealing with issues and

> Do you suppose the special education supervisor felt pressure from the administration for her alliance with Frank?

problems of any sort. The bus incident was just indicative of an overall ignorance of the issues. The special ed supervisor, by herself, had very little power in these matters. She was effectively cut off from the mainstream administration and listened to only when joined by a parent. We found that it took a joint effort to accomplish what should have been standard operating procedure.

In our state, IEP meetings for kids with behavioral problems are also, supposedly, attended by the county mental health authorities for a holistic approach. It was felt, rightfully so, that psychological help was needed in determining the best approach. However, in Greg's case, no one from the mental health organization ever attended any meetings. No matter how much pressure was applied, and there was a great deal, they just didn't bother. This particular school did not have an in-house counselor or psychologist and relied upon the county organization for these types of issues. It was clearly not working. In the end, we gave up trying to get them to attend. I often wonder what the outcome would have been had we actually banded together to help this kid.

By this time, Greg was a very angry and frustrated young man. He had been tested, retested, poked and prodded for most of his life. He had also become obsessed with weapons. He would fashion them out of large sticks or pieces of sharpened metal, lengths of chain, and he acquired knives of all sorts. When asked, he would say that they were for "defense."

Our relationship deteriorated rapidly. I was now the authority figure in his life, and he was determined to undermine it, at first with subtlety then more overtly. Incidents became more serious, with alcohol first and then drugs. Fights at school, and outright confrontations with teachers, became more frequent. Suspensions became more prevalent. Greg was at home more than he was in school. Several of the suspensions were for the possession of some sort of weapon in school. Due to his reputation for fighting, he said he needed the weapons at school to defend himself. All of my business travel came to a halt, and with it, more pressure from work. I just could not leave town without someone to care for and watch Greg. He was too volatile. This is where the county mental health people could have helped in terms of respite, a place for Greg to stay, or someone to stay with him, etcetera. The help was not forthcoming, the excuse being a lack of funding, lack of personnel, etcetera. The special ed supervisor and I tried various agencies with no success. An obvious option, at this time, was full-time care in a "group-home" environment. I, however, was too naive and perhaps a bit arrogant in my thinking. This was my kid, after all, and I should certainly be able to manage, and isn't it better to have a child in a home environment rather than an outside agency? I thought so at the time. My experiences show why parents of ADHD children need support and education. It's almost too much to handle with two parents, let alone one.

> Laws do not mandate mental health services, as they do special education services. According to Woodruff et al. (1999), while children's mental health services are still in short supply, there are a number of model programs where school and mental health agency collaboration is strong.

By this time, the company that I had been working for had closed their local facility. I had two choices—move to another state or accept layoff. I chose the latter, primarily because of Greg. I was determined to see him through high school in the same school. Some of it was self-serving. After all, I had laboriously spent 3 years building a support infrastructure for him at this school. The other issue was that I felt strongly about disrupting his high school years with a move. As it turned out, it made absolutely no difference. I chose to start my own consulting business and had long talks with Greg about what this would mean—working long hours at home, odd hours, traveling in-state to client sites, and reduced income. I asked him to economize on several things, citing the reduced income. I also asked him for more help around the house. Oddly enough, he took this well and actually did help out more, and he watched things like heating and lights.

THE NEXT FIRST OFFENSE

More attention came from the police, this time a Halloween prank instigated by Greg with two friends. They went out in a car playing "mailbox baseball." One drove and another leaned out of the rear window hitting mailboxes with a baseball bat. Greg, impulsive as he was, took "trophies," and brought them home and hid them under the house. At 10:00 a.m. one morning while Greg was at school, I glanced out the window and saw four police cars pull up. Then came the knock on the door with five or six police officers and a search warrant. They searched the entire house and found Greg's trophies. They asked where he was, I told them at school, and they wanted to go and arrest him there. I asked that I be allowed to pull him out of school quietly, and they agreed. This was officially a "first offense," as all the other incidents had been handled unofficially, so Greg was put into the Court Diversion Program. In this state, this entails a small fine, community service, and written apologies to the victims. Greg was given 75 hours of community service. Since he had no transportation, I drove him to each session. He performed this reluctantly and with poor grace, considering it a joke.

As it turned out, this was the first of three times my home was searched by the police. Each time, Greg managed to slide by in terms of penalty. There seemed to be a reluctance on the part of the police and the courts to actually give Greg a penalty that would make an impression. I have never, to this day, fully understood this attitude.

We had several confrontations, all verbal, about his behaviors. Several of them were quite bitter. He chose to ignore, or treat with contempt, any effort I made to understand what he was going through. Oddly though, regardless of his propensity toward violence and the intensity of some of our confrontations, he never lifted a hand to me. He never struck me, nor pushed me, nor even attempted it. I attribute that to the fact that despite his anarchical and contemptuous outlook, he recognized that I was his safety net, a place to stay in comfort. Basically, he knew a good thing when he saw it, and knew that physical violence to me would be the last straw. I remained his advocate all during the worst of his behavior, and he was contemptuous of that, feeling that I was a sucker. Greg does not understand and rejects affection and love.

Drugs were now a major part of Greg's life. He was dealing drugs out of the house, as I later found out during one of the three searches. Again, there was no action by the police or courts. He was slapped on the wrist again.

EXPULSION

Greg had become interested in computer-aided design and graphics due, in part, to my business. I always had computer equipment around, and while initially he used it for games, he became interested in creating designs and working with graphic arts. The school has a vocational program in graphic design, all on computers, and I had long discussions with him about his future. He was now almost 18. The special ed supervisor and I arranged for him to start the vocational program. It seemed ideal for him. It was something he liked to do, and it was focused upon a career path.

He lasted two months. He had gotten into a "personality conflict" with the director of the vocational program, an admittedly rigid personality. Greg flouted rules, of course, as he always has. This went against the grain of the director. While rules are a fact of life and Greg had to conform to some extent, the director would brook no infractions whatsoever. Greg was asked to leave the program, basically expelled. Greg did not, and does not, have the ability to see the viewpoints of others. If they don't behave the way he sees the world, he writes them off contemptuously. This was a major opportunity for him, and he basically blew it. He can also not see any further than the end of his nose, has no organizational skills with regard to his life, and believes that the future will take care of itself.

Now out of school, I told him that he needed to get a job and contribute to the household, go back to school full time, or move out. Those were his choices. Furthermore, his contribution to the household was to be 25% of his income. He made some feeble attempts at jobs, mostly seasonal work at the nearby ski resorts, washing dishes, prep cook, busboy, etcetera. These jobs were less than minimum wage, and his attempts to get other jobs came to nothing. He didn't have a high school diploma. The special ed supervisor and I tried to get him to acquire his GED with no success. His appearance and reputation, by this time, would have put off any employer. He contributed for awhile, then it became clear that he was spending most of his money on drugs. I called a halt. I had a long talk with him, the upshot being that the living arrangements were not working, and he had to find a place to live. He was now almost 19.

Eventually, he did move out, supposedly on his own. Every once in awhile, he would call and visit briefly, on his way to a friend's house in the area. I frankly felt a sense of anxiety whenever he called, wondering what was going to happen now. His visits were almost always about money, although he never asked overtly. I'm afraid that I used money and rides back into town as a method of getting him out of the area. He has had a series of part-time jobs, making enough, basically, to keep him in drugs, I think. He has lived with a series of roommates, almost all of them drug dealers. He has become a "street person" and is well known by the police.

There have been a series of incidents—an assault (dismissed), cruelty to animals (time served), and, finally, theft and smashing parking meters. It was shortly after his arrest for the latter, that he called from jail and assumed that I would pay his bail. I refused. This, of course, made him extremely angry. On his next visit up to this area, while I was out, he broke in and stole a handgun from my bedroom. He was the only person who knew where it was, and nothing else was taken, nor was the house disrupted in a search. Only my bedroom door, which was locked, was kicked in, and a footlocker, which was also locked, was torn apart. I reported the theft to two police agencies, in my own village, and in the city in which Greg lives. They did nothing. I find this appalling, due to the fact that a potentially volatile 19-year-old is now potentially armed. It's my impression that, due to my refusal to pay bail, Greg figured that I had now "written him off," and he was free to do as he wished.

This is how Greg thinks. His court date is approaching for the parking meter arrest, and his defense attorney thinks that he will get at least 4 months in jail. I sincerely hope that the court finally realizes that this kid needs to be brought up short, and soon. My feelings about jail time for Greg, however, are ambivalent. I fear that in jail he will learn how to become more careful the next time.

TURNING TO JEFF

> Now, at age 19, is Greg still salvageable? Do you know of adult services for him?

I recognize and carry a lot of guilt for my role in this. I had always thought that Greg was salvageable, that he wasn't really a bad kid, that ADHD clearly wasn't his fault, etcetera, etcetera. In my ignorance of the issues, I tried an approach that clearly didn't work. I am not an authoritarian person, and my egalitarian approach yielded no results, except contempt from Greg. However, I have no regrets. I did what I could.

The exception is one major regret. My other son, Jeff, too, is ADHD. He's 16 now. His case is far milder than Greg's, and for the entire period discussed he lived full-time with his mother, visiting us on weekends and during school holidays. Jeff is a much sweeter child and not prone to violence. He worships Greg, although he is beginning to see him for what he is. My regret with Jeff is that he got very little from me during these years. Greg demanded attention, albeit negative, and Jeff was just "there," demanding very little. My only excuse, although a poor one, is that I was always emotionally drained dealing with Greg. During the time when both of them were living with their mother and visiting only on weekends and school holidays, my time with them was spent as an arbitrator of fights, instigated primarily by Greg. I had to keep them at arms length, frequently separating them in other rooms. Greg picked on Jeff incessantly and violently, and to this day, Jeff fears him, even with the worship. I have reconciled my neglect of Jeff with him, having many long talks, and apologies. He and I have a good relationship now, without Greg in the picture, and share many things and good times.

I would say to any single parent of an ADHD child that you are in for a difficult time. But, it need not be as difficult as my experience. Proper coordination with schools and mental health organizations can do much to help. Unfortunately, you have to fight for it. My ex-wife and I should have started when Greg was very young. Perhaps things would be different now if we had. I found with Jeff that love and attention, along with the coordinated effort, works well. These kids are almost universally impulsive in their actions and cannot see the consequences of these actions. Rewards and punishments do not seem to work. They accept whatever they are given with equanimity. There was literally nothing with which I could penalize Greg, nor any reward that meant anything to him.

I have now become responsible for Jeff's education through an agreement with my ex-wife. Continual attention is needed, as well as good negotiating skills, to see these kids through school. This attention needs to come from the parents, the school, and outside mental health agencies, and it needs to be coordinated. The statistics show that most kids grow out of, or adapt to, ADHD, by the time they are in their late teens. This has not been the case with Greg, although it's now difficult to tell whether his problems are ADHD related or borderline sociopathic. Jeff, however, is another story. Medication for him is now much reduced, and he can get along well without it for extended periods of time. He's still somewhat cavalier in his approach to school, but a lot of that has to do with being 16, I feel. There's hope for Jeff—he has goals and plans, a good sign.

Activities

1. Prepare a list of the goals that you would expect to see on Greg's IEP at the point that Frank and the special education supervisor organized the first meeting.

2. *Discuss:* Greg's problems started at a very young age, and the doctor was the primary resource for this family. How might children be identified before school entry, who might be responsible for or assist in the identification process, and who could provide services to children with disabilities before they enter kindergarten?

3. Assume the role of a teacher in Greg's new school, where he has just started classes after moving in with Frank. Greg has been in your class for almost a week. Although you intended to write Frank a note earlier to say welcome, you have not yet. You have noticed that Greg is not getting his work done. In addition, you have realized that it is hard to get Greg to stay on task when you give him time in class, and he has not been good about turning in homework assignments. Write a letter of introduction to Frank. Use this opportunity to begin to establish a positive relationship with Frank, to tell him a little about yourself and your class, and to set the groundwork for collaboration on these early signs of trouble.

4. Using the scenario noted in activity 3, role-play a meeting or a telephone call to Frank.

5. *Discuss:* How would a teacher effectively discipline a student like Greg? Consider the fact that Frank says punishment does not work. Would threatening to call Greg's parents serve as a deterrent? If the school suspended Greg, how would a suspension affect the family? Would it change Greg's behavior?

6. Dinners out were such a problem for this family that eventually they stopped going out. How would you advise Frank to address this problem and to address the other occasions when Greg misbehaves?

7. Prepare a packet of materials on ADHD that are appropriate for Frank. Provide a rational for your choice of materials.

8. Conduct research about what happens to young adult offenders in your area. Are there special programs or services for them? Do young adult offenders receive remedial education services or special education?

9. Discipline has been the major challenge for this family. Write a one- to two-page essay that compares what you know about effective behavior management practices to what Frank and others did to manage Greg's behavior. What theoretical

approach to behavior management does Frank appear to follow? What could you have recommended and done in collaboration with Frank to make discipline more effective? Try to be as specific as you would if you were discussing these plans with Frank.

10. *Discuss:* Frank may appear to you as flippant or distant at times. Do you think this has been Frank's approach to Greg all along? Can you speculate about the events and circumstances that contributed to his attitude developing over time? What would Frank say about his current approach?

11. *Discuss:* Do you think the divorce of Greg's parents contributed to Greg's problems? Do you think Greg's problems contributed stress to the marriage?

12. *Discuss:* Almost one-third of the parents in one study said that their child did not sleep through the night on a regular basis, with a majority of these reporting that the behavior was cause for concern (Knoll, 1992). How could you protect a child who roams at night?

13. We did not hear from Greg's mother in this case, so we can only speculate on her reasoning in any given situation. Write three different explanations that she might give to the question, "Why did Greg go to live with Frank?" Share these explanations with others in your class to learn about the additional perspectives they may have considered.

14. *Discuss:* Do you believe that Greg might have been better off in a therapeutic foster home?

15. *Discuss:* What do you think Frank will do differently with his younger son, Jeff? What evidence do you see of this? Do you see behaviors or attitudes that may lead to some of the same conflicts with Jeff?

16. *Discuss:* Greg was expelled from school on several occasions. Discuss the laws and regulations that govern the use of expulsion or suspension of students for behavior that is caused by their disabilities.

17. *Discuss:* What were the characteristics that made the special education supervisor "excellent at her job" to this father? Why did it take so long for anyone to step in and advocate for this boy?

18. Describe the best practices that teachers and other helping professionals should use to assist this family.

19. Write an analysis of this case, drawing parallels from this case to (a) your own experiences; (b) theory and research from class discussions, course readings, and knowledge gained in previous classes; and (c) other cases in this book.

Suggested Resources

Larson, K. A., & Turner, K. D. (2002, June). *Best practices for serving court involved youth with learning, attention and behavioral disabilities.* College Park, MD: National

Center on Education, Disability, and Juvenile Justice. Available for download at http://cecp.air.org/juvenilejustice/juvenile_justice.htm

Dwyer, K., Osher, D., & Warger, C. (1998). *Early warning, timely response: A guide to safe schools.* Washington, DC: U.S. Department of Education. Available for download at cecp.air.org/guide

Fiedler, C. R. (2000). *Making a difference: Advocacy competencies for special education professionals.* Boston: Allyn & Bacon.

Overton, S., McKenzie, L., & Reese, J. M. (2002). *Reflective practice: Implementation of the First Step to Success model.* Norman, OK: University of Oklahoma. Available for download at darkwing.uoregon.edu/~ivdb/index.html

Walker, H. M. (1998). First steps to prevent antisocial behavior. *Teaching Exceptional Children, 30*(4), 16–19.

References

Knoll, J. (1992). Being a family: The experience of raising a child with a disability or chronic illness. In V. J. Bradley, J. Knoll, & J. M. Agosta (Eds.), *Emerging issues in family support.* Washington, DC: American Association of Mental Retardation. 23

Sprague, J., & Walker, H. (2000). Early identification and intervention for youth with antisocial and violent behavior. *Exceptional Children, 66*(3), 367–379.

Woodruff, D. W., Osher, D., Hoffman, C. C., Gruner, A., King, M. A., Snow, S. T., & McIntire, J. C. (1999). The role of education in a system of care: Effectively serving children with emotional or behavioral disorders. *Systems of care: Promising practices in children's mental health, 1998 Series, Volume 3.* Washington, DC: Center for Effective Collaboration and Practice, American Institutes for Research. Available for download at cecp.air.org/promisingpractices

If the Schools Had Their Way: Mrs. Jones's Story

Commentary: Mrs. Jones is a 50-year-old White woman and the mother of 17- and 23-year-old children, both of whom have attention deficit hyperactivity disorder (ADHD) with accompanying learning problems. Mrs. Jones has been a single mother for the majority of her children's lives. She does not receive child support from either of the children's fathers, and the children, Bob and Charlene, rarely see their respective fathers. Mrs. Jones is a nurse by training. She works two jobs, one full-time job with overtime, when it is available, and a second job on weekends to supplement the family's income.

Mrs. Jones has encountered many problems obtaining special education services for her children and, in general, she has been dissatisfied with the services they have received. Her complaints raise numerous issues that compel educators to examine their practices. As Mrs. Jones describes the problems she has encountered, her case demonstrates how repeated struggles may accumulate into a hostile perspective that educators neither care nor help. She is fed up and discouraged about her children's futures. At this point, each new teacher who approaches Mrs. Jones for the first time will encounter her pent-up hostility and negative expectations. A major concern for educators is to avoid a posture of defensiveness and consider the ways in which a teacher might turn the dynamics around to build a positive relationship. What can educators' learn from Mrs. Jones's story that might prevent other parents from developing a similar attitude?

BOTH TIMES

I have two children, both diagnosed with ADHD. The two children are similar yet totally opposite one another. Their classic similarities are poor self-esteem, lack of motivation, self-defeatist attitudes, and a bottomless cup of poor-me attitude you cannot seem to fill. They can smother you with it. They hate one another. Both are competing against each other for attention. There is 6 years difference in ages. They are opposite in that Charlene is good in all the reading skills and poor in math, while Bob is good in math and poor in reading skills.

My first child, Charlene, was diagnosed in the first grade at a private school. Her teacher was fresh out of school and had some knowledge of ADHD and what to look for. Based on the teacher's observations of my daughter, the school psychologist was asked to test her. Charlene was tested and diagnosed with ADHD. My daughter failed the first grade.

I couldn't afford to keep Charlene in this school, so she repeated the 1st grade in public school. She was treated for ADHD with medication by the leading pediatrician in the community working with children with ADHD. She was also receiving counseling for

ADHD by a licensed psychologist. Even with this documentation, the school would not accept her into special education. The school stated she did not qualify. What were those qualifications? No one seemed to know. She struggled along, barely passing, until she was finally accepted into special education in the 10th grade.

My daughter did graduate from high school. I am thankful that while there she did not get pregnant, did not do drugs, and did not drink. I am upset that she cannot seem to hold a job, she still does not have a good self-esteem, she still is a self-defeatist, and the school did not provide her with a good, proper foundation for her education and her future. Also, the schools undermine what a parent tries to instill in the child at home.

My second child, Bob, was diagnosed with ADHD in kindergarten. I had him tested privately by a licensed psychologist who said that he was far out of the normal category. Bob was also treated with medication by the same pediatrician as my daughter. My son repeated kindergarten because he did not master enough. He went on to the first grade, but I did not ask about special education. I was afraid of getting the same answers I had been getting for 6 years with Charlene. I was not looking forward to another fighting struggle. Bob had a tough year but was passed to the second grade.

I requested the school test him for special education at the beginning of the second grade. The school denied him. They told me he fell into the normal range category. I made a special trip to the school and demanded to see the idiot who had done the testing. I was very angry! The school retested him, and this time they agreed that he had dyslexia and was not in the normal range. He was placed in special education.

I do not believe the school was ready for a repeat of me. I could tell this by their actions towards me and especially the unspoken body language. Is special education worth the trouble? Who is it harder on, the parent or the child? I am thankful that so far he is not involved with drugs or alcohol. I am upset that he has not developed a good self-esteem, he still is a self-defeatist, and the school still does not provide a proper foundation for educating him for his future. Again, this whole process undermines everything a parent tries to instill in the child at home.

PROBLEMS WITH TESTING, PLACEMENT, AND MEDICATION

> Does your local school district make arrangements for its teachers and related service personnel to attend IEP meetings? What reasons might the school district offer for not accepting private testing?

I encountered a lot of difficulties in my children's education. One area is testing. I do not know what they test children with, but all children seem to fit into the normal category. I believe, if the schools had their way, there would not be special education programs. I resorted to using private testing by a licensed psychologist for my children. I did not trust the public school testing system for several reasons. First, everyone falls into their normal category. They won't show you their scores. They don't tell you what the scores mean. Also, they won't let you have a copy for your records even when specifically requested. I had to fight for them. They don't tell you what tests are going to be given. Finally, not all parties would show up for scheduled IEP meetings—they send substitutes. What do the substitutes know about what is going on?

My children have never qualified for special education through school testing. I have always had to provide private testing records if I wanted my children to get assistance. The schools did not pay for this private testing either. I always got flack for having my children privately tested. The schools do not like it. How dare I challenge them? I guess they felt I was a threat to them somehow.

Another problem area is medication. Schools are antimedication. They are adamant about what I need to do for them to receive medication at school, including a permission slip and documentation from the doctor. Then, the school would not remind them of medication. This was true for both children. They said it was the child's responsibility and the child's problem if they did not take the medication. How many children do you know that can remember to take medication, no matter how old they get? How much can a child do? With Bob, a lot of times there is not always a nurse or anyone else available at the time that he needs to take his medication. He gets down to the office and nobody is there or they say come back later. Then his teacher won't let him go again. Therefore, a lot of times Bob will miss it or wait and get into trouble from the teacher as well as the nurse or someone else for not being where he should be.

> What are your school's policies about administering medications? Are the people who administer students' medications trained about their personal interactions with the students?

Generally, the secretary gives the medication. Secretaries do not like it because it is not their job. Charlene was made to feel as though her medication was an imposition. If she was busy, the secretary would make all sorts of tacky remarks about her medication and her parents like, "You don't need it, you're just fine," or "It is just hurting you." Ultimately, the child won't take medication anymore. This is because the school has convinced the child that the parent and physician are wrong and she doesn't need medication. When you realize what is happening, it is too late. The damage is already done. That is what I mean about the school undermining the parent. It takes a long time to correct and regain that trust and confidence from the child about their medication. The medication is a learning aid. It is not a means by which parents can control and subdue. The parent has to learn to deal and manage when the child is not on medication.

Classroom placements were a problem too. As long as the schools followed the closed concept method of teaching, everything worked pretty well. ADHD children do not function well in an open-school concept. There are too many distractions. I faced the open concept with my daughter when she went to the seventh grade. That year was a real stumbling block for my daughter. She had a very difficult year. I began to petition the school board to change my daughter into another school district with a closed concept. This took almost the entire school year to gather documentation and set up meetings with the proper school board members. I got shuffled from one person to another. There was always a delay—lack of information, wrong kind of information, or the assignment of a new caseworker. These are great tactics to detour a parent into giving up the pursuit. I had to prove there was a need for her to change school districts through physician's documentation and licensed psychologist's documentation. The school board acted like we were lying and they just knew more than we did. Basically it all boiled down to the all-mighty dollar. It is about state-supported school money and the way it is distributed to the schools.

When the school board finally approved the transfer into another school district, they made it very plain that they would make no effort to help me in transportation to and from school. It was my responsibility to provide transportation at my expense. If I could not do that, then my daughter would just have to return and attend her home school regardless. My daughter went 2 years outside of her home local district.

TEACHER PROBLEMS, TOO

I admire anyone who has the patience and talent to teach and work with ADHD children. These children can really try your patience and skills in more ways than one. Still, I have had difficulty with teachers as well. Teachers will always tell you that they have on open-door policy, but that is not true. Teachers prefer out of sight, out of mind, and everything is OK, no problems. But, I think that they relate that to themselves, not the child. Teachers lie to parents. They tell you everything is fine, there are no problems, grades are good, and he or she is an angel. As a parent, I know different because my children are not angels, report cards do not reflect good grades, and all sorts of problems are listed under the comment section. Yet the teachers tell you everything is fine to your face. When meetings are held, cards should be laid on the table. The teacher and I should be there to discuss the child and how to help the child, a problem-solving session. It is a joint effort not a partial one.

> If Mrs. Jones' perception is correct, that teachers become defensive and see her as an irate parent, teachers and administrators might have difficulty putting aside their impressions and fears to listen objectively to the legitimate concerns that arise. What listening strategies could teachers and administrators use to improve problem solving and decrease defensiveness?

When meetings are held, scheduled or nonscheduled, several things happen. First, the teachers become defensive. They try to prove or protect themselves. Why? I was not challenging their authority or teaching methods. The teachers take the meetings as a personal attack against them. WHY? The teachers only know how to handle and deal with an irate parent. The teachers do not know how to handle and deal with a concerned parent. They are not trained for it, nor can they recognize it.

My children told me when they were having difficulty or something was going on that he or she did not understand or like, because my children were intimidated by their teachers. Usually their problems were legitimate, and I would ask for a teacher meeting. If they were not, we talked about it until he or she understood why it was that way and until they no longer had a problem with it. If we had a meeting, though, it was always the same. The teacher would get defensive, and not really listen. What she heard was an attack on her personally. I would try to explain how the child was perceiving the situation. Next, the teacher would assure me she understood and would take care of the problem. Then, my children felt picked on by teachers after parental conferences. The teacher, frustrated and angry, more at me than the child, takes it out on the child during school hours. This happens in a variety of ways. Sometimes, teach-

> From the teacher's perspective, what explanation might the teacher give for her actions?

ers make examples of the students, make fun of the student in front of their classmates, or embarrass them in front of the class. They do things like embarrassing him in front of everybody by saying, "OK, Bob, did you get all that?" Or, she would single him out by sending him to the board and say "Everybody, let's help Bob do this one."

Then the teacher denies taking anything out on the child. The teacher perceived this as taking care of the problem. Then why is the child so upset when they come home from school? This usually lasts for a period of 3 days after the meeting. This was an extremely consistent event. It could not be called a coincidence. It doesn't take many of these events to happen before the child is reluctant to tell you anything anymore. The tension caused by the meetings led to silencing my children rather than helping them. Ultimately, you have a teacher with blinders on, a frustrated child in school, and a frustrated parent dealing with this child who will no longer talk about school.

SPECIAL EDUCATION, FROM WHERE I SIT

> ARD stands for admission, review, and dismissal, and is a team meeting that develops and determines eligibility for special education services.

In elementary school, Bob's special education dealt only with major areas of disability and other classes were the same as regular classes. Moving from regular class to special education was not a big deal. The other children took it in stride, but still they had intuitive powers to know that Bob was different. I found general education teachers to be ignorant about ADHD. They had to rely on what information the special education teachers told them, and that portion is unknown to me. The special education teacher, if educated, has plenty to offer. For example, the special educator can suggest how to modify class homework assignments, class assignments, testing, etcetera. The more information a special education teacher can give to a regular class teacher who has an ADHD student, the better.

In middle school, our experiences there were relatively positive. The middle school my son attended had a different approach to regular class and special education. This school had a wing assigned for each incoming sixth-grade level. They stayed in this wing all 3 years. They had the same teachers, special education teacher, and counselor each year. The teachers along with special education worked together to develop teaching plans for special education students. Special education students would attend regular classes. Bob went to content mastery for 20 minutes of each class to supplement his teacher's instruction. I believe this has been an attempt to help educate regular classroom teachers to deal with and plan for special education students in their classes. It is not a perfect system, but a start. The regular class teachers really got to know their students, by working with special education teachers and student.

High school was a different matter. When Charlene was in school, there was no content mastery. It had not been developed. She was placed in special education classes according to her disability. I learned that special education is a farce. It is not managed on an individual basis. They are lumped together with children on various levels and different age groups. The teachers presented no challenge, no incentive to learn, and no positive feedback. The special education teachers did not care and were not interested in teaching. They were interested in primping or extracurricular activities that they were involved in with students. I saw a lot of favoritism, too.

> Content mastery is a model of service delivery that assigns a child to general education classes with additional help from a special education teacher on an as-needed basis. Often, the child remains in class for group instruction and then goes to content mastery for seatwork.

My son progressed up into a high school that uses content mastery but in a different format. Special education students are mainstreamed as much as possible. Content mastery is used for extra help. The ARD wasted no time in trying to dismiss Bob from special education.

He was doing decent, and they felt he no longer needed special education. I was so angry! Anyway, my son was not dismissed from special education.

I made several observations about high school special education. First, I noticed that the regular class teacher determines whether the student needs content mastery, not the student. Sometimes Bob would ask to go but was not allowed. I feel that special education students are different, not difficult to work with. They are a challenge, but most teachers are not looking for a challenge to use their skills. Teachers are not motivating special education students to improve their self-esteem. They do not always follow up with what they say they are going to do.

I feel I will be lucky if Bob graduates at the rate he is going. He may drop out of high school. Did you know that he could not even join the armed services unless he can show he passed through the 10th grade education level? That is a real shame when we have all these resources available. He is still going to school but not doing well. He may or may not graduate by the age of 20 years. He has ambition, but he seems to be lost in the education process of what it takes to get there.

> Parents of students 18 years or older are not prohibited from participating in IEP meetings if the child invites the parent.

It has now come to my attention that when Bob reaches the age of 18, as his parent, I can no longer attend ARDs. They will be completed by my son because he will now be considered an adult. He will have to handle his own affairs. I think this is wrong. As long as he has not graduated from high school regardless of age he is a minor and I as the parent am still taking care of his affairs. As I understand, Vocational Rehabilitation cannot even help him until he graduates. This is another stumbling block. What do I do now, but more important, what does my son do?

In conclusion, I wonder if it is all worth it. Who really cares? I do not believe that the teachers, schools, or society cares. Special education students are turned off. The parents get tired of playing king of the mountain and getting knocked down every time they get one step forward. There is always this constant struggle.

Part of our tax money goes to pay support for schools. A good education is owed, deserving of our children. They should not have to fight hard for a decent education. I believe my tax dollars pay for a good educational foundation, not high-priced police action baby-sitting for 8 hours a day.

Activities

1. Review the rights of Mrs. Jones's son, Bob. Pinpoint any situations that might exhibit a denial of Bob's rights or situations where you believe Mrs. Jones might be misinformed, unaware, or unclear of her rights. Obtain a copy of your local dis-

trict's explanation of rights for parents, and highlight the section that addresses pertinent information for Mrs. Jones.

2. Design a workshop for parents to acquaint them with their due process rights to testing, placement, and IEP development.

3. Assume that you are an advocate who is consulting with Mrs. Jones at the point that the high school team recommended Bob's dismissal from special education. Design an action plan for Mrs. Jones. Be specific about what Mrs. Jones should do.

4. Write a letter to Mrs. Jones, introducing yourself as Bob's ninth grade math teacher. What would be the most beneficial messages to convey to Mrs. Jones? What follow up to this letter would you plan?

5. Children and Adults With Attention Deficit Hyperactivity Disorder (CHADD) maintains that many children with ADHD are denied services because of confusion over eligibility criteria. In the regulations to clarify the 1997 reauthorization of the Individuals with Disabilities Education Act (IDEA), ADHD is specified as a health condition included under "other health impaired" when there is limited alertness to education due to a heightened alertness to environmental stimuli. Role-play an explanation of the eligibility criteria to Mrs. Jones.

6. Mrs. Jones believes that general education teachers have limited knowledge about ADHD. Develop a 1-hour presentation on ADHD, complete with handouts, for the teachers in your school.

7. Prepare a reading packet for Mrs. Jones that includes information on transition services, as well as information to help her son plan for life after high school. Be sure to include helpful information about eligibility for Vocational Rehabilitation in your state.

8. Compile two lists: (a) list the signs of a teacher's care and concern that a parent might see and (b) list the signs of a parent's care and concern that a teacher might see.

9. Conduct a search of the professional literature on the use of medication for ADHD. What are the most common medications prescribed, recommended doses, and side effects? What does the research say about the effectiveness of these medications? What are the recommendations about the use of these medications outside school hours?

10. Role-play the meeting that occurred when Mrs. Jones went to the school and demanded to see the "idiot" who had tested her son in second grade. Discuss how to handle confrontations when a parent is very upset with you.

11. *Discuss:* What is the distinction between an irate parent and a concerned parent? Mrs. Jones implies that she sees herself as a concerned parent, but she has been perceived as an irate parent. How do you think this discrepancy in perceptions developed?

12. Mrs. Jones is concerned about her children's self-esteem. What is the school's role in addressing Mrs. Jones's concerns? How would a teacher write an IEP goal to address this concern?

13. *Discuss:* How might a principal react to working with Mrs. Jones after several years of meetings that Mrs. Jones characterizes negatively? As you assign Bob to new teachers, what characteristics would you look for in a teacher to collaborate effectively? As the school principal, what information and advice would you give to Bob's new teachers? As a parent advocate, would your advice to Bob's teachers be similar?

14. Invite a guest speaker from an advocacy group who conducts workshops for families about educational rights and protections to discuss the frequent questions families have and the advice and training that the group provides.

15. *Discuss:* The concept of self-determination has been promoted to teach students to make and enact decisions and plans for their lives in order to gain independence. In high school, this often includes promoting student leadership in the IEP process. Should self-determination preclude a parent from attending an IEP meeting?

16. *Discuss:* Turnbull and Turnbull (2001) state that one element of a parent's motivation is hope for the future and that schools are more empowering when educators emphasize great expectations and positive outcomes. What are your expectations for Bob? How could you help Mrs. Jones envision greater outcomes?

17. Describe the best practices that teachers and other helping professionals should use to assist this family.

18. Write an analysis of this case, drawing parallels from this case to (a) your own experiences; (b) theory and research from class discussions, course readings, and knowledge gained in previous classes; and (c) other cases in this book.

Suggested Resources

Center for Mental Health in Schools at UCLA. (2003). *A resource aid packet on students and psychotropic medication: The school's role*. Los Angeles: Author.

Grayson, T. E., Wermuth, T. R., Holub, T. M., & Anderson, M. L. (1997). Effective practices of transition from school to work for people with learning disabilities. In P. J. Gerber, & D. S. Brown, (Eds.), *Learning disabilities and employment* (pp. 77–99). Austin, TX: Pro-Ed Publishing.

Podesta, C. (2001). *Self-esteem and the 6-second secret*. Thousand Oaks, CA: Corwin Press.

Online Resources

The Technical Assistance Alliance for Parent Centers offers the following handouts on parental rights, which are available from their Web site at www.taalliance.org/publications/index.htm: (a) Attending meetings to plan your child's individualized education program (IEP): Some suggestions to consider (2002); (b) Evaluation: What does it mean for your child? (2001); (c) Parent tips for transition planning (2001); (d) School accommodations and modifications (2001); (e) Special education evaluation (2001); and (f) Understanding the special education process (2001).

Visit the links on the Web site of Children and Adults With Attention Deficit Hyperactivity Disorder (CHADD) at www.chadd.org.

Also visit the Web site of the National Association of Protection and Advocacy Systems at www.protectionandadvocacy.com for information about local Protection and Advocacy agencies.

References

Turnbull, A. P., & Turnbull, H. R. (2001). *Families, professionals, and exceptionality: Collaborating for empowerment* (4th ed.). Upper Saddle River, NJ: Merrill/Prentice Hall.

CHAPTER EIGHT

El Puede Aprender (He Can Learn): Maria's Story

Commentary: Maria left Mexico with her mother 14 years ago, at the age of 28, to find work in the United States. Maria's two older brothers remained in Mexico, and Maria obtained a job providing child care for a family. After marrying and having two children, this soft-spoken but strong-willed woman left her husband because he mistreated their son, Renaldo, who has multiple disabilities.

An important facet of this case is Maria's faith and determination in her son's growth. Ignoring the predictions of professionals, and without training, she seemingly sensed how to stimulate Renaldo's learning. Maria attributes much of his progress to divine intervention, but she also correlates her son's growth to the dedication or the lack of dedication of his various teachers. Maria's story demonstrates how differences in expectations can cause friction. Additionally, Maria's story shows how fear and mistrust of the system can result in avoidance and can inhibit a parent from involving professionals in a search for solutions to problems.

Maria speaks Spanish, and this story is a translation, which lends importance to the story from that communication point, as well. When a teacher communicates with a parent who speaks a different language, a child, neighbor, relative, or another teacher usually serves as the translator, rather than a professional translator. When dealing with translations some frustrations can arise, such as atypical phrasings that raise questions about meaning and uncertainty about whether to attribute meanings to the speaker or to the translation. Maria believes that teachers seldom listen to her because she does not speak English. Although Maria has recently started to learn English, she says that her current ability is embarrassingly limited; therefore, she does not tell anyone. Maria's story demonstrates that deep and meaningful messages may sometimes unfold in a different, seemingly awkward manner. This translation of Maria's story will provide an opportunity to care enough to listen to ideas and feelings, and it will serve to stimulate a discussion of biases that arise from language differences.

FAITH

In this writing that I give, I begin the story about the illness of my son with the purpose of helping you. My pregnancy was normal until 5 days before the birth of my baby. During those 5 days I suffered from a fever. That's why I thought that the child would have problems at birth. The first 5 months were normal. We were at the zoo when he began to have a high fever. It was summer and I thought it was a light flu. I gave him medicine to calm the fever, but as soon as I gave it, he vomited. I took him to the doctor, and he told me that the fact that he had vomited the medicine indicated that this type of fever was very serious.

They put him on machines and took X rays. They didn't know what it was until one day they told me that the boy had meningitis and that his illness already was advanced. He had a fever of different degrees for 1 1/2 months. Later, it was complicated by pneumonia and seizures.

> Maria often refers to her son as "the boy." Does this seem strange? Contrary to what this literal translation might convey to the English-speaking reader, the Spanish word "el nino" does not convey an impersonal detachment.

The doctors said he would have to have an operation because he had too much liquid in his little head. In the operation, they put in a little hose which was the size of a piece of spaghetti. When he came out of the operation, he was blind. The doctors said that they were not responsible even though the operation was within his eyesight. On top of the lost vision, they told me that the operation did not have good results and that they had to do another the following week. They did the same operation for the second time, but in a different place. This operation had good results and the boy's vision recovered.

This is a touchy subject, but God provided for my son. During Renaldo's surgery, there was a stranger who saw me crying. He approached me and said "Why are you crying?" He couldn't speak much Spanish, but I learned that he had a daughter who was having open-heart surgery. He told me that my son would be taken care of, and I know this was God's message to me to have faith. The stranger brought me a Bible and brought his family to Renaldo's room. Even though I could not understand the words they were saying, I knew they were praying for me. It was only after the man prayed that Renaldo started seeing again.

Some hours before leaving the hospital, the doctors did an evaluation of the boy. They said that he would act like a 4-month-old child for the rest of his life, and that he wouldn't be able to do anything like walk, talk, eat, see, cry nor be able to physically move. I was to take him to a place for therapy once a week, and I wasn't driving at that point. I learned how to drive by myself.

> How consistent are your own religious beliefs with Maria's? What reactions do you have to Maria's faith, and how does this influence your impression of her? Why does Maria say that this subject matter is touchy?

On the way home, we heard on the radio of a man who had cured a little girl that had meningitis, but they didn't say who he was. When I got home, I called the radio station and they gave me the address. My mom and I took Renaldo, and we thought it would be a man like us. It wasn't until we got there that I realized it was a church, and the man that they were talking about was Christ. They said if you want your son healed, you need to accept Christ. As a mom you would do anything to cure your child; if that means you walk on your knees, then you walk on your knees. So I wanted to know Christ.

I started going to church, and at that church I offered him to God. I felt that if Christ had given me this child, he would help cure this child. In God's death he left the Bible, which is his word and his promises.

The boy was 6 months, and I continued to talk to him and he behaved as if he were more healthy than anyone else. I think this was very important. I was sure that my son could understand what I was saying. Even if a doctor says these children can't feel, they feel. And he was very aware of what was going on around him.

FAMILY

I was married then, but my husband did not help me. He was macho and thought Renaldo was trouble. A mama feels the children more, maybe because we carry the babies in our body. If Renaldo hurts, I hurt at the same place that he hurts. My husband thought I exaggerated, but it's true.

Renaldo was 2 years old when we had his brother, Carlos. My husband did not treat us well, though, so I split. I don't feel that children should be hit. Even Renaldo needs to be corrected, but not hit. Renaldo would be laying on the floor where he spent a lot of time, and my husband would come and kick him for no reason. It was difficult, but I took the children and hid from him. I did not have a future with him. His brothers and sisters all had homes and good things, but when I would talk to him about buying our own home, he would say that we couldn't because of Renaldo. He does not know where we are and we haven't seen him in years.

> Although Renaldo is only 12 years old, what does Maria's statement about preparing her younger son to be a husband imply about her expectations for Renaldo?

My younger son is 10 years now. My obligation with my own son is to help him develop. I talk to my little son a lot about only having one girlfriend, not many, and being a good husband.

In my life, I have switched roles for my children. The little one becomes an older child, and sometimes I think that is not right. If I go and take a shower, I will put the little one in charge. He's very smart and he knows how to take care of his brother very well. They'll put a movie in or something, so he's comfortable. The little brother takes very good care of the older brother. We have taught him that this is your brother and you need to love the brother. Also that he has to be of service to people and that he could not laugh at anybody. Since he was little, he had always been very attentive. If he sees you with a broom, he would bring the picker-upper. He is very independent. If he's hungry, he will make himself a sandwich. He is just a very independent person.

My mom and my niece live together in their own house about 10 minutes from our house. Since I have been on my own, my mom has really been helpful and supportive. I am the only girl and the youngest. I only went to school until sixth grade, and the things that my mom has taught me are the things that have been important to me—the school of life. I never lived with my dad.

My older brother was here for 2 years. Even though it wasn't Renaldo's dad, in those 2 years I could see the need for a relationship between a dad and a son and how much a child can grow in a relationship. He needed the relationship. My brother would take him out and show him things and play with him. He would put the pool outside and put himself on the same plane. He had to go back because he has his own two kids, but when he calls, he says "Take care of my children." Now, he worries and suffers because he can't be here.

I have another brother, who I didn't think liked my son. But now that my niece is here, I know that he suffered with me about this child, even though he's not here.

DEDICATION

When Renaldo was 2 years old, he began to have very strong seizures. He had 30 seizures a day and each one had a duration of 3 to 4 seconds. Myoclonic is the name of these seizures that my son suffered from. He would first raise his arms, open his eyes very wide, and have an accelerated respiration. They prescribed Dipekene, a medicine that he was taking four times a day to help him diminish the number of seizures.

When he was 3 years old he enrolled in a public special education program where he received occupational and physical therapy. This program lasted for 1 year. The physical therapy consisted of physical exercises like holding his head up or sitting. I was feeling happy with this teacher because I saw that she was interested in teaching, and my son made great progress.

The occupational therapy consisted of doing manual activities. I never felt comfortable with this teacher, and the boy did not respond. Miles away you could see that she wasn't interested or dedicated. Even though I am not an educated person, I'm not dumb; I can see these things. Like if you take a child's hand and make them touch and feel, and you show them that you want them to do it. With this teacher, even if she had studied for years, she just didn't show that. If you have a mother looking at you teaching her child, at least then you would be more interested.

When he was 4 years old, he attended the public schools, of where he also was receiving physical therapy and occupational therapy. There were 10 children with different abilities that were integrated in the classrooms with an array of disabilities. The teacher in charge was a young woman who was 25 years old.

The school was responsible for giving the medicine to my child, and the teacher in charge of giving the medicine did not do it. I knew this because he started to suffer more seizures than normal. I took him to have a blood test. The doctor said that the analysis indicated that the boy was not taking his medicine regularly.

A few days after, they called me on the phone to inform me that he had fainted at school. I went immediately to see what was going on with my son. Upon arriving, I found him very pale. I thought that he was like this because he had not eaten. I took him and gave him food, and he began to react.

The next day, I went to the school to talk to the teacher. I told them that the boy hadn't been taking his medicine regularly and had not been eating well. They knew that my son could not eat alone and that he needed help. They did not do much about this and told me that they did not know what was going on. In my opinion, this is a job where they need to be very responsible with the children.

On another occasion, some months later, my son came home with an eye injury. He could not open it for 2 weeks. I went to see what happened. They told me that he had fallen off a swing that they had lifted him to, and they had only left him alone for a few seconds. Perhaps he had a seizure at that moment or he simply fell off the swing.

I felt obligated to make an appointment with the director and the teacher so that I could discuss with them everything that had happened since my son started attending this school. I did not speak English at all at that time, so I took my police friend. Teachers do not pay any attention to you if you are not English-speaking. When you don't speak the language, they think you are stupid. So you have to come with someone who speaks English. They will listen then. There is a difference between not speaking English and being dumb. Just because you don't speak the language doesn't mean that you are dumb. You can think clearly in English and you can think clearly in Spanish.

The director and the teacher apologized, and said that they just didn't know what had happened. I don't know if it is true, but I heard that they took away the teacher's salary increase for 1 year. This made the teacher turn on my son and me. After that the teacher's attitude was very negative. She would come and smile and say "Good morning, how are you?" but I would notice in her face that she was very bothered and very annoyed.

At the end of the school year, they told me that he could not continue to be enrolled in this school and that he would have to change to another school. They did not give any reason why he would have to do this. I think it was because I had confronted them.

> What rights do parents have about placement decisions?

SURPASSING PREDICTIONS

My son was beginning to walk alone, supporting himself using the wall or some other furniture that was near him. At the new school, they gave him PT and OT like at the other school. The PT teacher was there once a week and told the aides what should be done with my son. He was supposed to walk through the halls using his walker every day for 20 minutes. This allowed him to strengthen his legs. He also would go up and down the stairs at home. He would first do this sitting down and then became more active.

They gave him swimming classes at school when he was just 6. There were only six classes in 6 weeks, and they taught him to float in the pool. The swimming teacher dedicated a lot of time to him. Later, I got a little swimming pool for the backyard. We would put him in the pool for hours and he loved it. It relaxed him and tired him, and then he would come in and take a little nap. It gave us a rest period too. Renaldo used to eat with his fingers because he could not support the silverware by himself. He would let you know what he wanted by pointing to it while making small noises. When I had to get him in and out of the car, or move him from one place to another, he would help me by following my directions.

In this school, when he attended class with the regular children, he didn't know how to behave. If he was near them, he pulled their hair and hugged them tightly. I think he just wanted to play and did not know how.

He continued to have seizures. Sometimes the seizures were provoked by loud noises. He could not pay attention to things going on around him. The seizures continued to last 3 or 4 seconds, and he would raise his arms, his eyes would open very wide, and his breathing became accelerated. I took him to the hospital and they hospitalized him for 1 month, so that they could treat his seizures. They tried different medicines to see which one would be the one that would give the best results.

One day, one of the students who came to the hospital took a blood test. She tried to find the vein in his arm five times without getting any results. It made me mad, and I did not allow her to do the test until a professional person came. This made everyone mad, but I was not going to let them practice on my son.

At the hospital, I already was noticing improvement in my son and the seizures were diminishing. When he left the hospital, I noticed he was more active and attentive. The medicine made his skin very sensitive and delicate, and he would bruise easily.

Every 6 months, they met with him to see how he was progressing. When he was 9, they made an appointment with me at the hospital to examine his legs and see if they could

> An electromyogram (EMG) is a diagnostic test, where the insertion of small electrodes into the muscle allows the doctor to measure the electrical impulses coming from the muscle.

help him walk better. Upon arriving at the hospital, they asked me to take off all his clothes and only leave the diaper. After that, they put wires in all of his body, but they put more wires in his legs. Then they made him walk to see if he had any difficulties. When they saw that he could walk quickly and not fall down, the doctors decided not to operate on him. He has a wheelchair but he does not use it very often.

He is able to open doors, and regularly he would leave class and walk down to the office. The teacher was getting tired of him leaving the class. One day he was punished and confined in a space marked with tape for an hour. His lesson was to learn about boundaries. She called and said that the next time that he left the classroom, she was going to call me to come down so they could whack him three times with a paddle. They were going to call me so I could witness it. I said OK.

> What part might culture play in Maria agreeing to the punishment, although she actually disagreed and made plans to avoid it? With the knowledge that Maria left her husband over his treatment of Renaldo, do Maria's actions surprise you?

That same day that she called, I witnessed how they paddled three other kids and I noticed that it wasn't a little piece of wood, a ruler; it was a thick piece of wood. When I saw that, even though I told Renaldo's teacher that it was OK for them to do that, I knew that if they touched Renaldo with that I was going to fall on the floor. I knew that if they called me, I would disappear and they couldn't touch him. I got caller ID, and when I saw who it is, I didn't answer.

They took my son down to the principal so they could punish him, but they could not get a hold of me. The principal did not dare do anything without my permission. I hope that no teacher ever does this. Maybe I would agree if it was a wooden spoon, but not with that piece of wood.

FAMILY SUPPORT SERVICES

An agency has paid a caregiver to help me with Renaldo for the last 3 years. I applied through United Cerebral Palsy, but I don't know why because he does not have cerebral palsy. One program says how many hours you need, but another program actually writes the check for my money. I applied and waited 4 years on a waiting list.

When they told me that I was going to have someone come and help, I thought that it would be better if it was someone that knows him, knows his habits, those things that only the family knows. Like he likes to get into the tub with his clothes and take a bath, or he likes candy. I decided to wait until my mother qualified as a caregiver. I didn't want anybody else to come. They told me there had to be two people, so they would alternate, but I told them no, I only want my mom. My mom took a course at the Red Cross on first aid so that she would qualify to take care of him.

For the first 2 years I was in the program, they gave me about 20 hours a week. As he grew older, I asked for more time, because as he is growing older, he can't do a lot of things. You have to be like face-to-face with him all the time. If not, in one moment, he will take all the spoons out, throw the pots and pans. Now, during the week he has 4 hours, but on weekends he has from 9:00 a.m. to 9:00 p.m.

They have a registered nurse come only once a year to do blood pressure, etcetera. She talks a lot with my mom and gives her tips. When the agency comes, they say that he hits them, but that he doesn't bother my mom. The agency asks her how Renaldo behaves, she says "Just fine." "Does he hit?" "Never." Anytime they ask her questions, she makes it sound like there are no problems, because she knows they're monitoring that and she is afraid they would change them. I know of a case where they got rid of a kid because they found out that he mistreated the caregiver.

Renaldo does not hit you so that you have to go to the doctor, but I don't think that the agency would like to know that he hits. My mom teases that she knows that people put cameras on baby-sitters to see how baby-sitters hit children, so she should put a camera on so people can see how the baby hits her. She laughs, "You give me the money and I will go to Las Vegas, because it's a lot of work taking care of him."

LATINO SUPPORT GROUP

I belong to a group of Latino mothers with handicapped children. We meet once a month for 2 hours. We all take coffee and fondue. Once every couple of months we have a doctor or psychologist or social security or school people talk to us, like what are your rights. You establish relationships. You talk about other things like, my daughter is 12 years old and she has a boyfriend. After 7 years we know each other very well, like who has a boyfriend.

| For assistance in finding a nearby support group, parents can visit the Pacer's Alliance Web site at http://www.taalliance.org or the NICHCY Web site at http://nichcy.org. |

But we don't visit often just because we are all very busy because of our children. We call on the telephone sometimes. For example, the group leader might call and say someone died and they call each other and go to the funeral and give support and money or whatever needs to be done. Or the leader will call and say somebody's kid is in the hospital, and we all have a kind word for each other. They are Latino in that sense, that if someone says I need company or something like that, they are there. Among ourselves we will say, X this happened to Y. Why don't you give her a call.

With the people in the group it is the same feeling, that you understand what they are talking about. If someone from the church calls and I say, I am tired, I didn't sleep last night, they really don't understand. But if another mom of a special child calls, they can say, "I know," because they have been there and they will say something like, "Why don't you bring him over so you can sleep." They understand. They won't understand unless they have a child like that. God forbid, but that's the only way people understand.

EVALUATIONS

He is now 12 years old. He attends a public school near our house with classmates who have different disabilities. He has one teacher and three aides. He continues to take 20-minute walks down the hall, he has swimming lessons and occupational therapy classes, he attends a regular class for 1 hour, and he goes on field trips. They are teaching him to dress and eat by himself.

My son weighs 86 pounds. He is a healthy boy. He eats well and is not sick from cough, flu, etcetera. The only thing he doesn't do is talk, but he is very intelligent. He can say, "mom" and "I love you" and we try to do that with him a lot. When he arrives at the house after school he eats in his chair. Now he eats by himself without needing anyone to help him. He knows how to use a spoon. When he wants water, he gives me a glass, and when he finishes drinking water he throws away the cup. After the food, he takes a quick nap for about 25 minutes. When he gets up, the first thing he does is turn on the TV. Already he knows the difference between videos and television programs. At 5 p.m., he already knows that the aide that works with him in the afternoons will be arriving soon. He begins to change clothes because he knows that they will be taking a walk in the park. If the aide does not arrive on time, he gets mad and cries loudly. When the teacher arrives, he recognizes her. He knows what he has to do when he is with her, like washing his hands without the teacher saying anything, getting a towel to dry his hands and throwing it in the trash when he is done.

The thing he likes the best is to ride in the car. Also, he already knows the streets where he lives. When we go out together and he wants something to eat, he signals me with his finger and begins to make some sounds so that we can stop. Now he knows the places where the food he likes is sold. He prefers french fries. When he returns, he undresses and goes to the bathroom because he knows that they are going to bathe him before he takes his favorite toys out to play.

Last year, they did an evaluation that said that he had the behavior of a 9- to 12-month-old child. In the evaluation that they did this year, they said that now his behavior is that of a 2- to 3-year-old child and that he is progressing quickly. I used to cry because the baby wouldn't do anything, sit, cry, or anything. Then he started to move, and sit up, and walk, and now I cry for joy. We laugh together. I keep telling him that "You have such a nice mom, and she loves you so much, and your mom is a beautiful lady" and he laughs and thinks that I am crazy.

I am grateful to God, because in working with other families whose children had meningitis, Renaldo can do things that other children can't do. God is still alive. One of the most beautiful things that has happened to me is that I had Renaldo, even the way he is, because instead of us teaching him, Renaldo teaches us. Renaldo teaches you to go on. An example is he will fall on the floor and he will get up and go on. He doesn't get sad, but we get sad.

Activities

1. Reflect on and write about the effect that cultural and language differences had on your understanding of this case, and include the following points.

    • Do you have any way to know which unfamiliar phrases or choices of wording were a cultural or language difference and which were probably indicative of this mother's individual personality traits?

- What cultural influences do you see in this case?
- What impressions did you form of Maria, and what was the exact wording of the passages that contributed to those impressions?
- How much of the sentiment conveyed in the case may be related to the translation?

2. Conduct research to find support groups within your community for parents or siblings of children with disabilities. Call various disability organizations and locate at least three parent or sibling support groups that meet regularly. Develop a directory that includes each group's name, the name and telephone number of a contact person, the frequency and location of their meetings, and a brief description of what occurs at their meetings.

3. Cite the occasions and methods of Renaldo's communications with his mother. Write an IEP goal for communication that would build on these communications.

4. Renaldo has far outreached the doctors' predictions for his future abilities. Write an essay relating this case to the research literature about low expectations threatening to limit a child.

5. *Discuss:* What criteria does Maria appear to use when she distinguishes between good and bad teachers?

6. *Discuss:* Does this school system provide an "educational context" that empowers families, as described by Turnbull and Turnbull (2001)? What opportunities are utilized for partnering with Maria? Cite the occasions when professionals fulfilled their obligations for reliable alliances.

7. Conduct research on Medicaid waiver programs, such as the program that pays for Renaldo's home attendant. These programs sometimes are called *Katie Beckett waivers.* Who is Katie Beckett? Does your state have such a program? Who is eligible for this program, how does one apply, how long is the waiting list, and for what services does the program pay?

8. *Discuss:* Was Maria in a "stage of denial" when she continued to treat her son as though he had not been ill? Turnbull and Turnbull (2001) state that hope is an important coping mechanism for families. It has been stated that teachers and doctors frequently give "false despair" rather than give "false hope." What are the dangers of false hope? What are the benefits of maintaining hope?

9. Advocacy can take many forms. Cite the occasions when Maria was an advocate for her child, Renaldo.

10. Organizations increasingly are publishing their brochures in multiple languages. Prepare a packet of readings in Spanish that address Maria's needs.

11. *Discuss:* What is the appropriate use of punishment? What, if any, parental permission must you have to paddle a child. You might wish to role-play or discuss how you would collaborate with parents to decide what consequences you will use with their child. How would you incorporate these plans into the IEP? Must you put these plans into an IEP?

12. How could you use the information that Maria provides to inform your assessment of the child's skills? Outline, in a bulleted format, the information provided about Renaldo's current level of performance. What would your next steps be to determine the family's priorities for IEP goals?

13. *Discuss*: Turnbull and Turnbull (2001) discuss the ways in which families draw support from various sources, including spiritual beliefs, practical and emotional support from friends and family, and assistance from professionals and agencies. Discuss Maria's sources of support.

14. Maria said she believed that people are thought to be less intelligent if they do not speak English. Interview an English as a Second Language (ESL) teacher to obtain information about the teacher's perception of bias in schools.

15. Reflect on the role that religion plays in supporting this family. What other ways might religion influence or support a family? How might religion, either your own or the family's, impact your role as a teacher?

16. Describe the best practices that teachers and other helping professionals should use to assist this family.

17. Write an analysis of this case, drawing parallels from this case to (a) your own experiences; (b) theory and research from class discussions, course readings, and knowledge gained in previous classes; and (c) other cases in this book.

Suggested Resources

Bazelon Center for Mental Health Law (2002, November). *Avoiding cruel choices: A guide for policymakers and family organizations on Medicaid's role in preventing custody relinquishment*. Washington, DC: Author. Available for download at http://www.bazelon.org/issues/children/publications/TEFRA/stateoptions.pdf

Beach Center on Disability (2000). *How to deliver services to Hispanic families who have children with disabilities*. Available for download at www.beachcenter.org

Family Voices (n.d.).) *Waivers: The Katie Beckett waivers and the 1115 waivers*. Available for download at www.familyvoices.org/fs/ma-kbw.html

Gallagher, P. A., Fialka, J., Rhodes, C., & Arceneaux, C. (2002). Working with families: Rethinking denial. *Young Exceptional Children, 5*(2), 11–17.

Lynch, E., & Hanson, J. (1992). *Developing cross-cultural competence: A guide for working with young children and their families*. Baltimore: Paul H. Brookes.

Smith, R. M., Salend, S. J., & Ryan, S. (2001). Watch your language: Closing or opening the special education curtain. *Teaching Exceptional Children, 33*(4), 18–23.

Southwest Educational Development Laboratory (2000). *Family and community involvement: Reaching out to diverse communities*. Austin, TX: Author. (ERIC Document Reproduction Service No. ED449248) Available for download at www.sedl.org

Online Resources

Visit the Epilepsy Foundation Web site at www.efa.org for information for teachers about seizures.

References

Bedford, H., de Louvois, J., Halket, S., Peckham, C., Hurley, R., & Harvey, D. (2001). Meningitis in infancy in England and Wales: Follow up at age 5 years. *British Medical Journal, 323,* 533.

Turnbull, A. P., & Turnbull, H. R. (2001). *Families, professionals, and exceptionality: Collaborating for empowerment* (4th ed.). Upper Saddle River, NJ: Merrill/Prentice Hall.

CHAPTER NINE

A Direct Ride Home: Shelly's Story

Commentary: This case presents a cry for help. Shelly, a mother of three, is in her 40s and is of Jewish descent. She has one son, Brian, with autism and mental retardation and another son with Asperger syndrome. Dissatisfied with Brian's lack of progress at school, this mother left graduate school and assumed the primary responsibility for home schooling Brian. She views the hours that Brian spends at school as her only respite. Shelly and her husband have both been ill, and she is near the point of exhaustion and overwhelmed with the financial and physical burden of doing what she believes is necessary. Shelly wrestles with the option of residential care and worries what will happen to their sons when she and her husband are gone. She explains how seemingly simple matters, such as transportation, can sabotage educational programming and family priorities. This case provides an opportunity to examine how school arrangements have a collateral effect on family life. In addition, this case challenges the reader to confront Shelly's perception that she must provide her son's education because educators are not trained adequately, they cannot be bothered, or they are caught in the middle. This case also raises questions about a teacher's risks and responsibilities when school decisions are in opposition to their professional judgment.

I COULD BE YOU

My name is Shelly, and I live in a suburb that could be Anywhere, USA. I have been married for nearly 20 years, and I have three children, ages 15, 10, and 7. My husband is a professional, and I am a homemaker. We live in a four-bedroom colonial with a large lot, beautiful shade trees, and a wooden swing set in the backyard. We chose our neighborhood for the excellent reputation of the school district.

I've run into other families in our quiet suburban neighborhood who have discovered that a child has special needs. It is hard to know just how many families there are, as many feel stigmatized, and all are protected by confidentiality. Yet, it seems from casual gossip that a surprising minority of families in our area are involved in this sort of struggle. The families of the more mildly disabled typically either negotiate with the school district or send the child to any of a number of excellent private schools in the area.

Sometimes, there is a special education school that is suitable for a particular child, and the family or the school district will pay tuition at that school. The large number of private schools, including special education schools, in our area has meant that many districts have not developed in-house expertise, or interest in keeping children in the least restrictive

According to the U.S. Department of Education (2001), over 68,000 school-age children with disabilities were placed in private schools by their parents in the 1998-1999 school year.

environment. Some families are able to shrug their shoulders and pay privately for all manner of tutoring and therapy that is redundant to that offered by school personnel, so that their children can keep their heads above water. Others hire an attorney and go through the IEP process. They find themselves caught in this wringer before they know what has hit them. And the experience can be quite nasty, sometimes for a number of years.

I have a daughter who is 7, whose only exceptionality seems to be giftedness. There are so many issues that I have with my school district, that I have decided for now to keep my daughter in private school for the next year or two. It is expensive, but peanuts compared to the costs of educating her brother.

My 15-year-old, the oldest, carries a diagnosis of mild Asperger's, gifted, global apraxia, and secondary depression. He has never been in special education classes, although I have had some very strained relationships with his schools over the years as a result of my refusal to place him in special classes. He has gotten support services in the mainstream, where he has always been an excellent student in all subject areas without academic modifications. He will be starting at the high school in the fall. Although he is a very gifted and accomplished student, and now considered well-behaved by school staff, he could not get into any private schools in this area that would provide appropriate academics. I am keeping my fingers crossed that things will continue to go well for him in high school.

My middle child, the 10-year-old, has severe autism and severe mental retardation. It is difficult to describe what it is like to live with a school-aged child with severe autism. Many of the small tasks of everyday life, such as shopping for groceries, going to the dentist, attending school events for other children, reading the paper, and so forth, take an enormous amount of planning. We do not have any access to respite care, as my so-called "natural supports," aka extended family, do not understand why he has not been put into residential care and are not willing or able to be trained to provide respite care. My parents are getting older and not in the best of health, and I need to help them out at times. It has been several years since my husband and I have even gone out to dinner or a movie together.

And then there are the bigger tasks, such as arranging for school. Going through the IEP process can be as traumatic as dealing with the disability. Even areas that should be as trivial as transportation can become major stumbling blocks. Allow me to explain, for example, the difficulties involved in arranging transportation for Brian.

OFF TO SCHOOL

When Brian was barely 3 years old, he began to attend the special needs preschool housed in our neighborhood elementary. He became the first member of his family to board a school bus. His older brother had always shunned the special education bus, as he was tired of the stigma of being a special ed kid. Lots of regular education kids were transported by parents, anyway, as the regular education buses were often very wild and disorderly, with minimal training in crowd control for the drivers. But, with different arrival and departure times for the two boys, a bus ride for Brian would certainly be convenient. He was not acutely aware that he did not ride the same bus as classmates or that he was different and deemed lacking.

We began by sending Brian home by bus. We learned that he cried the first day, but soon adjusted to the ride. Then, we added the morning bus ride. Although the school was

> How could naps negatively influence sleeping patterns?

only 10 min away, the ride took nearly an hour. Still, the extra time added to a short school day provided me much needed time with his infant sister. Brian was not sleeping well at night, and he soon learned to sleep on the bus. I did not even begin to guess that the daily naps might have aggravated his sleep problems. I enjoyed the brief respite provided by school, and felt confident that school attendance meant that his deficits were being addressed.

This type of ride was provided for the next 4 years, through an additional three schools and a move to a different state. Brian continued to sleep on the bus and wake during the night. On occasion, we would wait for lengthy periods of time for the bus, and by the time Brian arrived at school he would soil his clothing. His teacher would make harsh remarks about parents who neglected the teaching of personal hygiene. Unlike other small children with autism, however, he remained quiet, clothed, and buckled in while in transit. We had worked hard to eliminate disruptive behavior while in a moving vehicle so that we could safely take him places.

HOME SCHOOLING

> ABA means applied behavior analysis, which utilizes the principles of behavioral learning theory.

The hope of the early years receded as Brian did not make any credible progress during these years and became increasingly disabled, in spite of glowing reports from school personnel. Finally, when Brian was 7, we removed him from school to try an ABA intervention at home, to see if he were truly incapable of making any kind of progress.

Our first step was to attempt toilet training. After he was trained day and night, we went full-speed ahead with other basic skills, such as imitation, receptive and expressive language, and matching. We taught Brian to pump his feet on swings, and to stay with an adult on walks in the community. We taught him table manners. We taught him effective alternatives to disruptive behaviors and stigmatizing self-stimulatory behaviors.

We worked intensively, one-on-one, for at least 6 hr each day, with weekly consults from an autism professional experienced in teaching basic skills to very disabled autistic adults. Brian's language skills began expanding rapidly, and he achieved meaningful IEP goals for the first time ever.

DIRECT TRANSPORTATION

After a year of this, we agreed with our district to begin Brian at a local private school that specialized in autism. He would go to school from 9:00 a.m. to 2:00 p.m., and continue home programming in the afternoons and on weekends. We felt that he needed to get out of the house and among peers. I, too, needed a break. This particular school would take new students only up to the age of 8, so we couldn't wait long if we wanted the option.

We requested direct transportation as Brian gets carsick after long rides. We also requested a trained aide to handle behavior on the bus, as we were nervous that he would use excessive time spent in transit to practice self-stimulatory behaviors or to sleep. Additionally, after all the time and energy spent developing both good passenger skills and good imitation skills, we did not want him traveling with peers who would scream, disrobe, wander about the bus.

Once the first week of school rolled around, my heart sank. Apparently, the district transportation director was not privy to our agreement. She announced that a district bus would be picking Brian up in front of our house, and driving him to the bus depot of a neighboring district. He would then board another bus and backtrack through our district to get to his private school. There would not be an aide, even though he would be riding with another child who screamed so much that one of his bus drivers reportedly filed for workmen's compensation, saying that it had hurt her ears. We were told the entire trip would take 45 min. In shock, I agreed to try.

In reality, the trip took them 1 hr 15 min. Brian lasted 3 days. The first 2 days, he arrived home with holes chewed into his shirt, groggy from a nap. He was not awake enough to benefit from our afternoon home program, but he seemed to get a second wind at family bedtime. The third day, Brian staggered off the bus and threw up.

I called the director of transportation and asked that he be given direct transportation, as agreed upon by the director of special education. I suggested that the second bus pick up Brian on the way back through the district. Transportation refused to budge. I alerted my attorney, who was present when settled with the district, and I began to drive Brian myself. The trip took 20 to 25 min, one way.

> Analyze how these paragraphs inform us about Shelly's goals and how she assesses and programs for Brian's needs.

In some ways, I really enjoyed driving Brian. I was able to maintain the passenger skills he needs to participate in typical family outings, as well as to achieve some interaction during the ride. If he started to chew his shirt, which happens once every few days, with me, I stopped him immediately with various techniques. I discovered he takes great pleasure in picking out audiocassettes to play along the way, and that he thinks it is funny to pass traffic that is backed up along an exit. He catches my eye, points, and giggles.

In the afternoons as he waited for me to pick him up, he enjoyed "dancing" as he balanced along the curb of the parking lot. I tried to plant a "surprise" for him, usually a small toy, on his seat. One day, I was a few minutes late, and school staff told me he was crying "Mama" when I didn't show up. So, I tried to leave about 15 min early, so as to get there on time. He arrived home in the afternoon with time to have a snack and climb on the swing set, and play with me without competition from siblings before beginning his afternoon program. He went to bed at a reasonable hour and slept through the night.

On the other hand, driving Brian meant that I was on the road for 2 hr per day. This left me with very little free time, as the school day in this private school lasted only 5 hr. Free time was especially valuable to me as I was unable to access much respite, and Brian needed round-the-clock supervision during the time he spent at home. Even the tutors I hired to work with Brian needed frequent feedback. I had counted on at least having time to catch up with doctors' appointments and household duties put on hold during the year

Brian was home. I was unable to schedule appointments, including an IEP meeting for my oldest child, without a great deal of difficulty.

Then, my car broke down. I could no longer drive Brian to school. Nor could I take it to an auto shop and wait with my disruptive child for several hours while the car got fixed. So, Brian missed a few days of school, until I could find a respite worker to stay with him while I took the car in for repairs. Soon after, I was in a minor accident. Fall would become winter soon, and I didn't like the idea of driving in the snow, either.

Meanwhile, my lawyer was playing endless telephone tag with the special education bureaucracy. Although several individuals involved at school were confused and support- ive of my requests, they were caught in the middle and could do little. I was urged by other parents to complain to the state, or even file for due process. In hindsight, though, I believe that had I prematurely gone to the media, the school board, or the state, as several parents urged, I could have alienated potentially supportive people in the dis- trict. Teachers and even administrators sometimes get asked to go along with things that go against their professional judgment.

> If you were Brian's teacher, what would be the pros and cons of getting involved?

Finally, my attorney reported back to me that I would be getting a call from the spe- cial education director. She called later that day and promised that Brian would be given direct transportation. True to her word this time, a station wagon arrived within a few days to take Brian to school. The driver, a senior citizen, was able to bond with Brian almost immediately. He insisted that Brian buckle his seat belt himself, and chastised anyone who stepped in to thwart this sign of independence. This was one load off my mind. But, the process of getting to this point was unbelievably wearing.

EXHAUSTION

> From the district's view- point, what was the danger of acknowledging the ben- efit of the home program? Why would Shelly desire the school district's acknowl- edgment?

I am continuing Brian's home program that takes up about 40 hr per week. I hire the consultant and workers, so that I need only do about 20 hr of tutoring myself. There are many more prep hours involved. My district resists acknowledging that Brian has received any benefit from our efforts. Nevertheless, we are teaching him to read, to spell and type, to do simple math, to communicate through picture exchange, to talk, to follow household chore schedules, to groom him- self, and to use free time productively in a number of recreational activities. I sometimes say, half-jokingly, that I find myself having to become the profes- sional that the real professionals cannot be bothered to become. Formal school actually functions as little more than respite hours. I am getting very discouraged, as they do not have the expertise to do very much with the children, good intentions notwithstanding. They will follow through somewhat with instructions and material that I send in, but I think they are in dire need of direct coaching. I cannot do this myself, as it is too far from home and I have too much to do.

My husband and I have both had health problems, sometimes at the same time. My doctor says it is related to prolonged stress and exhaustion. My husband works long hours, and has a physical disability that often leaves him in a lot of pain when he is at home. At one point, my husband was hospitalized on an emergency basis, and he was also in a car accident that could have proven fatal. I am not at all sure what happens to my family if I go under. We have no friends or family who are willing and able to care for the boys.

I take some comfort in talking with other families. Weary families trade war stories, home remedies, and tales of small victories with others who can put themselves in the same shoes, who will not judge, and who will not expect to make small talk about the amenities of middle-class life that are closed to so many of us. Darker tales of family discord, divorce, physical and psychological decline among immediate family members, and such, circulate as well. Many families have given up expecting much from schools.

The school district has hinted that a residential placement would be OK with them, in lieu of all the bickering over appropriate services. My husband and I have resisted this, because we feel it would be very cruel to send such a young child away from a family and home that he obviously loves, especially as we have found that he can indeed learn adaptive behaviors when training is sufficient in quality and quantity. And we are reluctant to abandon the home program already in place for a program that would not necessarily provide experienced or trained staff or supervisors, judging from the experiences of other families. So, we really feel that we have no choice but to purchase services on our own, until we either run out of money, our community offers help, or I become very ill.

But, we do have some nagging questions about the matter, as we struggle to figure out how we can afford it all. We are going through our life savings and I expect that we will run out of money in about a year. Other parents have warned my husband and I that if we decide to keep Brian at home, at our expense, we may find access to group homes closed off once our child reaches adulthood, with preference given to children of parents who placed them early. What if we become ill or our financial situation changes and we cannot afford the home supports necessary? I often feel as if I am stuck in a situation in which I need to choose between bankrupting my family, putting up with substandard services, or relinquishing my child to a residential situation that I cannot influence.

Activities

1. Asperger syndrome is a pervasive developmental disorder that is characterized by a significant impairment in social interaction and the development of restricted and repetitive patterns of behavior, interests, and activities. It is described by many as an autistic spectrum disorder. Conduct a search of the professional literature and write a brief essay on the difference between Asperger syndrome and autism.

2. Interview a teacher of a self-contained, special education class about the children's transportation. Ascertain whether the children follow the same school hours and arrive at school on time, how long the children are on the bus, and how teachers' work with the drivers to handle individual behavior problems.

3. The Individuals with Disabilities Education Act (IDEA) defines transportation as a related service provided when the IEP team decides on the need for special transportation to enable the child to benefit from an education. Invite a bus driver or the transportation director to your class to discuss the issues that they must consider when scheduling buses. What method do they use to determine bus routes? What is the school district's policy about the maximum time a child should spend on the bus? How many bus aides does the school district employ? What training does the school district provide to bus aides?

4. Conduct research on the residential schools in your area. What populations do the residential schools serve? Determine how many children are living in residential centers and the percentage of payment for which the school district is responsible. Who is responsible for the payment of the remaining portion?

5. As the importance of respite care becomes increasingly recognized, more organizations, such as some local United Cerebral Palsy and Easter Seals offices, are beginning to sponsor respite care. The Camp Fire organization has a nationwide program that trains members to provide respite. Determine who provides respite care in your area, what the cost is, and what parents must do to schedule care while they go to a movie.

6. Read about the controversy surrounding various home programs that parents establish for their children with autism. One place to start is with the 1997 special issue of *Behavioral Disorders, 22* (4).

7. Reflect on and write about the effect of Brian's home program on the lives of each of his family members. In addition, speculate about the effect on the family members' lives if Brian did not receive the home program.

8. Arrange a tour of a residential facility for children.

9. Shelly obtains support from other parents on the Internet. Lists of Web sites that focus on disabilities are available at www.kidsource.com, www.pacer.org, and numerous other sites on the Internet. Research other Web sites that might be of interest to Shelly, including discussion groups.

10. *Discuss:* What needs would children with various disabilities have that might require transportation on special buses?

11. Can you identify certain decision points or places where the decisions made or peoples' behaviors had an impact on the course of events? In situations where decisions and behaviors had a negative effect on collaboration, how might a different handling of these situations produce a different outcome?

12. Research how guardianship is determined upon a parent's death. How might parents provide, through estate planning, for the future of their adult child with disabilities?

13. *Discuss:* Shelly feels that educators are caught sometimes between the political realities of being an employee and wanting to help families. How can teachers and administrators effectively advocate for parents when their judgment differs from an administrative stance?

14. Describe the best practices that teachers and other helping professionals should use to assist this family.

15. Write an analysis of this case, drawing parallels from this case to (a) your own experiences; (b) theory and research from class discussions, course readings, and knowledge gained in previous classes; and (c) other cases in this book.

Suggested Resources

Fickes, M. (1998). Caught in the middle. *School Planning and Management, 37*(3), 44, 46, 48.

Fiedler, C. R. (2000). *Making a difference: Advocacy competencies for special education professionals.* Boston: Allyn & Bacon.

Myles, B. S., & Simpson, R. L. (2003). *Asperger syndrome: A guide for educators and parents* (2nd ed.). Austin, TX: Pro Ed.

Simpson, R., & Zionts, P. (2000). *Autism: Information and resources for parents, families, and professionals.* Austin, TX: Pro Ed.

Spence, B. (2000). Long bus rides: Their effect on school budgets, family life, and student achievement. *Rural Education Issue Digest.* Charleston, WV: AEI, Inc. Available for download at www.ael.org/rel/rural/pdf/digest1.pdf

Online Resources

Visit the Web site of the Autism Society of America at www.autism-society.org for information and resources concerning autism.

In addition, read about the controversy over ABA training in the special 1997 issue of *Behavioral Disorders, 22*(4).

References

U.S. Department of Education. (2001). *Twenty-third annual report to Congress on the implementation of the Individuals With Disabilities Act.* Washington, DC: Author.

CHAPTER TEN

Straighten Up:
Ms. Stack's Story

Commentary: One professional after another attributed Ms. Stack's accounts of her son's behavior to what they perceived as her own mental health problems. Rather than accept the diagnoses and recommendations for counseling, Ms. Stack continued to search for someone to see her son, Ryan, as she did. She determined from her own research that Ryan had Tourette syndrome, but for years no one—teachers, psychologists, or doctors—believed her. Ms. Stack longed for support, but it appears that the more desperate she became for help the more others were convinced that she was the problem.

Were all of these professionals ill-informed or predisposed to parental faultfinding? Ms. Stack's words are emotionally charged, presenting a crisis that professionals do not see, and her thoughts seem to jump around. Ms. Stack might also convey the belief that she knows more than the doctors. This 42-year-old White woman is a single mother who has limited family support and lives what appears to be a very stressful, dangerous, and chaotic life with her son, Ryan. Her story reflects the chaos of her life, both in the situations described and in the storytelling. This case provides an opportunity to develop a deeper understanding of the ways in which the dynamics of communication might influence professional judgments, as well as a parent's receptivity to help.

I LONGED FOR CLOSURE

My son is 12 years old and has been diagnosed with Tourette syndrome, obsessive–compulsive disorder, ADHD, nonspecific depression, and intermittent explosive disorder. For any parent, the knowledge that your child has been born with some type of disability is devastating. However, the majority of these parents learn fairly early in their child's life that something is wrong and are able to begin the grieving process. For others, it becomes a nightmare. Obtaining an accurate diagnosis for Ryan was the complete antithesis. It took many years of conflict, hospitalizations, altercations, and research to finally gain the support we needed in order to begin the extensive and painful process of medication trials. The search for this diagnosis became the grieving process for me. I longed for closure.

The most aggravating element of this ordeal was that I already knew the probable cause of his dilemma, but was ignored solely because I was the parent. Before Ryan was finally diagnosed with Tourette's, all the projections over the years had been anxiety disorder or separation anxiety. They weren't so far from the truth. I guess I can't really blame them during the early years, because the tics hadn't manifested themselves yet, and they saw Ryan under the best of circumstances. He was highly manipulative and able to suppress his tics for hours at a time.

By far the most disturbing element was the accidental discovery concerning Ryan's civil rights and the many different forms of assistance that were available to him. I felt an extraordinary sense of betrayal. The inordinate effort, time, and exceptional frustration that went into finding help for him on my own could have been erased if those who knew that the services were available had directed me to them. Our lives would have been just that much easier. The issue is that schools and state agencies don't go out of their way to advertise assistance, because it becomes an issue of funding.

> According to the American Psychiatric Association (2000), Tourette syndrome involves motor tics, such as eye blinking, tongue protrusion, touching, or squatting, and one or more vocal tics, such as clicks, snorts, throat clearing, or uttering words. The most commonly associated symptoms are obsessions and compulsions, but hyperactivity, distractibility, and impulsivity are also common.

THE DISTRESS DOESN'T EASE

I always thought things would stabilize after awhile and our lives would become smoother. On the contrary, the fluctuations of symptoms were so unpredictable and constant that the distress doesn't ease up for a minute. Now with Ryan having reached puberty, the ever-changing and progressive aggravation of his symptoms seemed to rekindle the trauma of years ago.

Entering sixth grade, a middle school, the stress of yet another and larger school, Ryan's anxiety and tension increased. The most irritating circumstances were the struggles that went on between me and school personnel. For instance, in sixth grade, the lead special education teacher had a son with Tourette's. Apparently, he didn't have any behavioral disorders. This particular teacher, who also had a great deal of weight in the ARD, kept telling me, on occasion, that she had never noticed any tics. Well, over the years, my son became very astute at suppressing his vocal and motor tics. The minute I picked him up from day care, he felt safe with me and the tics were explosive. They continued on for hours at home. The noises and movements were overwhelming. Ultimately, this teacher came out and basically declared that she didn't believe he had Tourette syndrome and that she would know because she raised a son with the disorder. Halfway through the school year, I received a call at home from this teacher who was aghast and nonplused that while in her content mastery room that day, she watched Ryan for an hour when he finally couldn't hold the tics back any longer. She talked and talked to me that night, but never apologized, just justified her actions and opinions because she had never experienced anything remotely similar to this.

Ryan was physically ill throughout the school year, so much so that he was homebound near the end of sixth grade. The same thing has appeared this past year, although it started around December, probably because he felt more comfortable at the beginning of the year. His tolerance for any anxiety is minimal. One of the many symptoms that emerged very quickly in life was school phobia, a common trait in children with Tourette's.

> How could you, as the teacher, help Ms. Stack to cope with Ryan's school phobia?

Most administrators, teachers, diagnosticians, and especially the kids, don't understand that anxiety and fear usually manifest as psychiatric problems. Getting Ryan to school, even day care, was and still is a monstrous task. Most times, while he was younger it was kicking and screaming every school day. As he became older, it manifested itself in physical illness. Very real illnesses, confirmed by physicians every

time. Being highly sensitive to everything (including clothes), Ryan had no way of dealing with the teasing, put-downs, slowness in learning, the outbursts and hyperactivity,
etcetera. These were not just by the other kids but many times by the teachers themselves.
He avoided school like the plague. He had no friends, and when he began to find them,
there would be an incident in which he lost them. He got into many fights, usually trying
to defend himself.

When Ryan started the seventh grade, we had moved from the city's school district
to this smaller suburban district. Even though Ryan still had numerous problems to contend with, there was a vast difference in the way the ARD committee approached his needs.
There was a more notable sense of empathy and desire to assist us, due to the small size of
the school district. The teachers, administrators, and psychologists were all very supportive as well as realistic. In the other district, there had been years of
grievous disappointment and struggle with each different school that
Ryan attended. My attempts to obtain services, especially their support, understanding, and flexibility in meeting his needs, went
unheeded. There was an embedded sense of desensitization and hard-
ening concerning kids with behavioral disorders. The schools ruled
firmly with ideas of conformity to modern rules and regulations of
our society. Strangely enough, I found the approach and punishment
of these children harsher than what criminals receive. Criminals have
their rights fiercely protected until proven guilty, yet children who
need desperate understanding and help seem to be discarded so
effortlessly. There was no room or place for unusual or uncommon
measures to help a child through the educational process, one that
was already very frightening for Ryan.

The issue of control was addressed by Knitzer, Steinberg, and Fleisch in a now-classic 1990 report for the Children's Defense Fund, *At the Schoolhouse Door: An Examination of Programs and Policies for Children with Behavioral and Emotional Problems.* Their report concluded that "too often the dominant curriculum is not the tradi-tional academic curriculum, nor is it about concepts, thinking, and problem solv-ing. Instead, the curriculum is about controlling the behaviors of the children" (p. 25).

He was put into every placement available and nothing worked.
In most cases, I found the teachers wanted nothing but control in their
classrooms. In many ways, I understood their feelings, but there were
very few who made the attempt to work with me in setting up exceptional methods of helping Ryan fit into the classroom setting.

A MISUNDERSTOOD DISORDER

The most part of Ryan's life has been harsh. Tourette syndrome and all its associative disorders is possibly the most complex and least understood disorder. Most people, teachers,
friends, even my family still want to believe that he can stop what he's doing and "straight-
en up." Tourette syndrome and obsessive–compulsive disorder (OCD) thrive on anxiety
and fear. Every day I remind myself of how he thinks and try to respond to that particular
moment. Most of his fears are chronic to the point of phobia. Most of our conversations
revolve around reassurance that "No son, that car is not following us home. We aren't
going to be kidnapped or hurt." "Ryan, this is our back porch and even if it's dark, we're
safe. There isn't any killer out here who wants to butcher us." It's very difficult for others
to understand how deeply fixed this fear goes. It is beyond imagination, and to most, probably absurd. My son has never sat directly on a toilet seat, even though he watches me
scrub it for him, because "there might be even one tiny germ and then I'll get a disease and

The combination of Tourette syndrome with the onset of adolescence was something even I didn't expect. As a professional therapist and parent of a child with a severe neuropsychiatric disorder, I set out to develop a strong knowledge base about this condition. As much as I've read and researched, I can probably challenge most physicians about what makes him behave the way he does in any given circumstance. I have delved deeply into the clinical, emotional, and neuropsychological aspects. Yet, despite everything I know, the very heart of life with a disabled child is that I live in my child's existence moment to moment, day to day. I'm the one who's always there, not the doctors, or anyone else. This in itself bestows parents an intimate and instinctive wisdom that no other individual will ever be able to identify with or comprehend.

However, no matter the knowledge or understanding that I have accumulated, and the belief that I've encountered something new that will help Ryan, the unpredictability of this condition still leaves me feeling lost, in utter despair, and helpless. From one moment to the next, Ryan experiences, out of the blue, single or combination episodes of severe mood swings, extreme hyperactivity, loss of impulse control, and motor and vocal tics, to include utterances of obscenities and socially and personally inappropriate actions.

> It might be tempting to speculate about the ways in which this family's life might be different if Ryan's father was living at home. What alternative male role models might be available to Ryan?

Being a single parent has also made this more difficult in many respects. Without a male role model, my son is having a very troublesome time adjusting socially to new and confusing feelings about his sexuality, girls, and friendships.

ASSOCIATIVE DISORDERS

With Tourette's comes the associative disorders of ADHD, and OCD. The obsessive–compulsive nature leaves him without the ability to control most impulses. For many years there were episodes that were usually very dangerous. One that stands out for me is the year we lived across from a park. There were so many times when I couldn't locate Ryan because he had vanished so quickly. I was always frantic. He was 9 years old but intensely immature for his age. He ran across the street in front of our apartment, where speeding cars are ceaseless, and over to the park. He found a lighter and began to ignite it under the park benches, putting the flames to the palms of his hands. He had no control. He never does.

Recently another episode happened in which he was wandering around the apartment complex and found matches. The next thing he found was a bag. In a split second the bag was on fire. Unfortunately, the police and fire marshals were called. I paid the $62 fine which was meant to discipline my son. The absurdity of this episode was the court clerk exclaiming that she had to look up the fine for illegal burning of trash because the city hadn't issued the citation in over 10 years.

Other things that I had to learn to live with included his need for "the right feeling," which can be described as ritualistic behavior. If Ryan was watching a video and I said something to him or tried to move, he was compelled to restart the video. It took four restarts for me to recognize what was happening. He also needs to arrange things in an exact pattern. In addition, he has the unfortunate compulsion to pull his hair out until he actually becomes bald. I began to cut his hair very short, yet under stress or feeling tired, he continues to do so. Including mine. This is rare and known as trichotilimania.

Common in a diagnosis of Tourette's is "intermittent explosive disorder," or rage attacks. When he was young, I could hold him in a bear hug for usually an hour until he calmed down. He became self-abusive during these episodes and it was up to me to keep him from hurting himself. As he got older, stronger, and bigger, they became much more difficult to manage. This all began at the age of 2 when my ex-husband moved our family back to this area for a job offer. Six months later he was gone. The move itself for Ryan was traumatic, but the loss of his father has never left him. It was at this age that he began banging his head against walls, cement floors, doors, anything hard. He never felt the pain until later. He has no memory of the rage attacks, the time was a blackout for him. He hit out at anything or anyone in sight.

Over the years, countless windows, property, toys he loved, his own body, and me, have been battered. I have replaced three car windshields. If he happened to "go off" in the car, I couldn't get off the road fast enough. He was already trying to jump out of the car. He was suicidal and homicidal during these attacks. I was so physically abused, black and blue from trying to stop him, that I had to make the most difficult decision in my life. The first time you commit your child to a psychiatric hospital is the most devastating. I felt like a complete failure and the guilt was overwhelming. It never goes away. But then neither does the screaming madness you feel inside. Sometimes, hate borders with love because this child commands your life, leaving you empty, seriously questioning your belief in God.

EARLY YEARS

I knew shortly after birth that something was seriously wrong. For the first 2 years he never slept more than 1 hr at a time. He was colicky, contracting many colds and what appeared to be allergic reactions. I suffered 2 years of sleep deprivation. He was and still is on antibiotics almost every other month for some type of infection.

> What do you know about measurement theory that might help explain Ryan's IQ scores dropping over time? How would you explain this to his mother?

There were blissful times. He was a happy baby most of the time, and had an infectious laugh. The one constant throughout the years of psychological evaluations, placed Ryan's IQ in the superior range. The first IQ was 140, but with anxiety and constant retesting his scores gradually lowered due to test anxiety.

He is extremely intelligent, thoughtful, and fascinated by the metaphysical. He asked many questions at a very young age regarding the beginning of time, God, and spirituality. Another story that will always stand out for me was Ryan's question to me at the age of 5: "Mommy, what was there before the universe when there was the blackness? Was there another God and another universe?" He actually started talking at the age of 6 months. We were astounded one day to hear him say "Wha dat?" while pointing to every item in his sight. This happened with neighbors, my parents, his paternal grandmother, and family members. I always answered his questions. At age 2, we were bringing home 25 library books a week. I noticed quite early however, that he did seem to have trouble applying this knowledge to paper and pencil tasks. The vast difference in his intelligence and the ability to apply it practically is still pronounced. Up until last year, he couldn't tell the difference between his right and left hand. I repeatedly gave him cues that would help him but to little avail. He's just now learning, at age 12, to know the difference between his right and left shoes. You don't lose your patience with problems that appear simple enough for a five-year-old. You simply accept and continue to teach and help him understand.

PSYCHOLOGICAL EVALUATIONS

The first attempt with psychological evaluations was through a private center that is well-known and respected locally. Ryan was less than a year old. They completed a thorough examination. However, only one short visual observation was made of Ryan while playing in an office saturated with children's toys. Once focused on something new, Ryan becomes concentrated, quieter, displaying very few of the actions that happen at home. In the final analysis, the team told me point-blank that once I straightened out my life, Ryan would follow suit. The written recommendations included: "emphasis was placed on Ms. Stack to obtain mental health counseling as soon as possible."

Six years later, when he was 7, it was recommended that Ryan again be evaluated. He tested at a private agency. Not once did Ryan or myself speak or meet the master's degree therapist. The summary stated that he was only an overanxious child and that family therapy with mother should be addressed as soon as possible.

The third evaluation was initiated by Ryan's second-grade teacher. Once again, the foremost recommendations was that "mother be referred to parenting guidance center to improve bonding" and "Ryan's mother should be encouraged to follow through with securing therapeutic assistance." Again, this was completed by a master's level therapist. The hint of probable ADHD was finally addressed, primarily by the observations of the teacher.

For the next several years, I just tried to live with everything, watching Ryan closely for a change in behavior that I hoped the Ritalin, Cylert, and related drugs would bring about. It never did, and we became enveloped in the controversy of whether or not Ritalin can cause the onset of Tourette's. It is my own feeling that Ryan was predisposed to it genetically.

When Ryan was 11, I was able to track down the Tourette Association. There was absolutely no doubt in my mind that Ryan was experiencing all the symptoms of Tourette syndrome. I acted swiftly on this. I was referred to a renowned neurologist in our area, a member of the National Medical Board for the association. He was finally diagnosed with Tourette syndrome and was started on medication. The potential side effects of these drugs can be dangerous as we found out. We ended up in the emergency room at least twice due to severe complications.

With diagnosis in hand, this doctor referred us to a child psychiatrist, as he felt the behavioral problems should be handled by the psychiatric community. Disaster followed. Every psychiatrist completely dismissed the diagnostic report by his neurologist. One of the doctors simply wouldn't see Ryan after about 5 min in his office and deemed him a probable psychotic. Another seemed to care less, and another was clueless as to what to do. At this point, Ryan had become dangerous to himself and others. We were slowly withdrawing the use of Ritalin that was causing severe motor and vocal tics. Still, there were no proper medications to control the multiple symptoms he was experiencing. I made the decision to admit him to a prominent children's hospital in the city. The director of child and adolescent psychiatry was his physician. Upon admission, my son's examination was fairly accurate. But the discharge notes sums up the resistance and barriers I have encountered with the medical and psychiatric community since the beginning of this pilgrimage.

> He was angry, distractible, highly irritable. Thought processes limited, thought content filled with worries and fears that his mom and he would be harmed. Thoughts of death and suicidal ideation. His affect was irritable, mood volatile and dsyphoric. He was highly agitated, crying and bargaining with his mother. But no motor or vocal tics were noted.

After one week, he was discharged. The discharge report stated

> Mother was convinced that he has Tourette syndrome and wondered about other conditions as well. The behavior described at home was not observed in the hospital setting, although he was highly active, restless, difficulty with attention and fearful at times. There was no neuropsych deficits characteristic of Tourette's except for attentional difficulties. Mother continued to be quite concerned about him, she seemed at times to add more symptoms she had noted over the years. We recommend that the mother not change from doctor to doctor, no further neuropsych testing. Mother needs to stop embellishment and encouragement of symptoms in child. Recommend the use of amphetamines, but mother refused fearing the use would cause an increase in his tics. Mother was very disappointed and upset that the patient was not kept for a longer period of time in the hospital and that a diagnosis of Tourette's was not made.

> Why did Ms. Stack not take the recommendation that she stop going from doctor to doctor? Can you isolate words or phrases that Ms. Stack might have found offensive?

One more neuropsych evaluation was developed on the recommendation of a highly respected neuropsychologist whom I knew personally. It was bizarre and based on a comparison of Ryan's assessment to that of a norm-based study "with a group of children with TS and ADHD. Evidence of neuropsych deficit is lacking based on the data of the study. Neurological disorder is not a very promising rubric for understanding Ryan's behavior." It was at this point that I went $800 in debt to purchase a camcorder for proof of the motor and vocal tics. The footage was excellent and helpful in the final psychiatric evaluation.

We reached the beginning of the ending of this nightmare this last year when Ryan had to be admitted again to a psychiatric hospital. This time, the clinical director of the children's unit held Ryan in the hospital for 3 weeks and stated

> This patient has a supportive mother, although she is somewhat overwhelmed and acknowledges past history of dysfunctional relationship with her son. An extensive history of Ryan confirms Tourette syndrome. As Ryan's anxiety increased, it was clear that any anxiety-provoking subjects elicited increased aggression and upper-extremity, shoulder, neck, and facial tics.

This physician took the time to listen to me and consider the research of medications that I thought might be beneficial to Ryan. He agreed. He also felt that my son very possibly had Tourette syndrome from birth due to some of the very unusual symptomology present. It took 12 years to secure the medical support and confirmation of my son's condition.

I HAVE NO IDEA OF THE FUTURE

I think the most painful insight that I've had with my son was recently during an intense disagreement when he said "If you knew what I was going to be like, you would have had an abortion." I was stunned and shocked to find out that he felt that way. There are so many things that I still don't know about him. I try to talk with him, but these are troublesome years to communicate with a teenager.

But Ryan and I have had wonderful times together. We spent years at the playground, playing games together, watching movies, going to museums, all the usual things that families do. At the year-end ARD at school recently, the teachers were so impressed with Ryan's ability to maintain himself despite the overwhelming odds, they all felt that he could try going to regular education classes next year, mix amongst his peers and find new friends, and learn better coping mechanisms and manners of interacting. This was the last thing I expected. I was excited and proud, yet a little frightened. I probably don't give him enough credit because of what I know so intimately about him. In our home he feels safe enough to release pent-up emotions and urges, but some of that is happening in public now and they are major concerns. I also must admit that it's been very hard to find humor in my life these past years. I feel like I've lived a lifetime already, but when I watch my son sleeping at night I close my eyes, kneel beside him, and reaffirm that tomorrow we can start again.

> What types of help does Ms. Stack need with Ryan at home? What services does Ryan need at school? Would it be appropriate to reflect these needs in an IEP?

The one story that I carry with me, the one that makes everything worthwhile, is the day several years ago in the dead of winter. The skies had turned dark and black with rainstorms approaching rapidly. Ryan was outside somewhere. I was worried about him because he had disappeared again. The rain came down in sheets, thunder and lightening lit the skies, and I was on my way out to find him, when he came running in the house sobbing and deeply distraught. I'd never seen him like this before. He was able to tell me his story. He was coming home when he saw a young man of about 18 swaying strangely with sudden jerking movements, walking in the middle of the street. As the boy came closer to the sidewalk, Ryan, who is usually deathly afraid in these situations, attempted to get the boy off the street. He guided him by the hand to safety. I suspect that the boy was mentally retarded or even schizophrenic. The boy, still acting strangely, asked Ryan if he thought it might rain soon. By this time it was pitch black outside and the storm was reaching its height. Ryan began to cry softly. He took off his jacket and put it around the boy's shoulders. This mysterious young man just smiled at my son and walked away in the bizarre, rambling way. Ryan ran home, deeply concerned and troubled for the continued safety of this young man. We never saw him again. My child was acutely distressed for many months, he continued to cry for him. So much like a story called *The Star Thrower,* I know that my son, somewhere within his soul, "labors to understand the nature of nature," of his own disability and the questions of his life. I, though, already understand his goodness and who he is. I am, as so beautifully worded by Max Van Manen "possessed of a passion" that only a parent can know.

I have no idea of the future, let alone today. My greatest fear is that my son will put himself, unknowingly, into a dangerous and life-threatening situation. But then again, he could triumph and experience what everyone hopes for in life—a good job, a family, friends, and happiness. We have far to go and it seems like forever, but he is my child and I will do whatever is necessary to help him find this.

Activities

1. As Ryan gets older and bigger, his mother discusses new challenges in dealing with his behavior when he gets out of control. What types of services does this family need to stay together and grow? Make a list of at least five resources for Ms. Stack, including addresses and telephone numbers, and explain how the organization or agency could help her. How would you begin to collaborate with these organizations or agencies to help this family?

2. Reflect on the feelings of screaming madness, hate, and love this mother describes. These feelings are described as a result of dealing with Ryan, but they are now also a part of the relationship between Ryan and his mother. Write a paper that relates these feelings to the research on family dynamics.

3. Ms. Stack relates two occasions when Ryan set fires. Visit, or invite as a guest speaker, a therapist or administrator of a residential facility or group home for individuals with psychiatric problems. Do they admit clients with a history such as Ryan's? What is the course of treatment for a child who sets fires?

4. Mrs. Stack mentions that her feelings sometimes make her question her faith in God. Search the professional literature about how religious beliefs support parents. Do family members use ministers, rabbis, or other religious leaders as support systems and, if so, what types of support do these individuals offer? In addition, conduct an informal survey. Call three clergy and ask whether they have had experiences in counseling families with a child who has disabilities.

5. Highlight the words in the case that carry special emotional content. Analyze and discuss Ms. Stack's choice of words. Did her word choice influence the impression you formed of her?

6. Role-play the telephone call from the teacher whose son had Tourette syndrome, explaining that she had observed Ryan's tics for the first time that day. Discuss whether a straightforward apology is necessary and appropriate.

7. Conduct a search of the professional literature on school phobia to determine the most common and effective course of action. Determine how you would represent this action plan in Ryan's IEP, including the statement of current level of functioning and goals and objectives. Address what Ms. Stack perceives as students teasing and initiating fights with Ryan.

8. How do you think Ms. Stack would characterize the components of an excellent evaluation process?

9. Professionals blamed Ms. Stack for years before the confirmation of Ryan's diagnosis. Read about the interactional–transactional model of family influence in Kauffman (2001, p. 238). Then discuss in a brief essay the manner in which Ms. Stack's behaviors could have been affected by not being believed and being seen

as the cause of her son's problems. Do you think that Ms. Stack's behavior was influenced by Ryan's behavior?

10. *Discuss:* Was Ms. Stack's opinion that professionals do not tell parents about assistance because of funding valid?

11. *Discuss:* It has become increasingly common to hear calls for parents to be responsible for their children's behaviors. Ms. Stack's fine for the fire that Ryan set is such an example. Would this fine be effective in producing a change in Ryan's behavior or would it be ineffective?

12. *Discuss:* Does this family need family therapy? Why was Ms. Stack unwilling to accept professional recommendations to obtain counseling? Was there an approach to the recommendation for counseling that might have been more effective?

13. *Discuss:* According to Gaffney and Ottinger (2000), it is thought that while an individual may have some control over his symptoms from seconds to hours at a time, the suppression of those symptoms may merely postpone more severe outbursts. What factors might account for Ryan's behaviors being so different at home and school that the school did not see his explosive behaviors and tics?

14. Compare the content and tone of the passages of the reports that Ms. Stack quotes.

15. Describe the best practices that teachers and other helping professionals should use to assist this family.

16. Write an analysis of this case, drawing parallels from this case to (a) your own experiences; (b) theory and research from class discussions, course readings, and knowledge gained in previous classes; and (c) other cases in this book.

Suggested Resources

Center for Mental Health in Schools. (2003). *A resource aid packet on students and psychotropic medication: The school's role.* Los Angeles: School Mental Health Project—UCLA. Available for download at smhp.psych.ucla.edu

Forness, S. R., Sweeney, D. P., & Toy, K. (1996). Psychopharmacologic medication: What teachers need to know. *Beyond Behavior, 7*(2), 4–11.

Kauffman, J. M. (2001). An interactional–transactional model of family influence. In *Characteristics of emotional and behavioral disorders of children and youth* (7th ed.). Upper Saddle River, NJ: Merrrill/Prentice Hall.

Miller, P. A., Ryan, P., & Morrison, W. (1999). Practical strategies for helping children of divorce in today's classroom. *Childhood Education, 75*(5), 285–89.

Online Resources

Visit the Web site of the Obsessive–Compulsive Foundation at www.ocfoundation.org for information on obsessive–compulsive disorder.

In addition, visit the Web site of the Tourette Syndrome Association at www.tsa-usa.org for information on Tourette syndrome and related disorders.

References

American Psychiatric Association. (2000). *Diagnostic and statistical manual of mental disorders* (Rev. ed.). Washington, DC: Author.

Gaffney, G. R., & Ottinger, B. (May, 2000). Tourette syndrome. *University of Iowa Health Care Virtual Library*. Retrieved May 13, 2003, from www.vh.org/Patients/IHB/Psych/Tourette

Kauffman, J. M. (2001). *Characteristics of emotional and behavioral disorders of children and youth* (7th ed.). Upper Saddle River, NJ: Merrill/Prentice Hall, 238.

Knitzer, J., Steinberg, Z., & Fleisch, B. (1990). *At the schoolhouse door: An examination of programs and policies for children with behavioral and emotional problems.* New York: Bank Street College of Education.

Growth and Adjustment: Grace's and Janet's Stories

Commentary: Janet and Grace are mother and daughter. Their stories intertwine, as do their lives with one another and with Jake, Janet's younger son with physical and hearing impairments. Disabilities affect the whole family, as this case demonstrates. In addition, this case illustrates the ways in which teachers can have a positive or negative influence on an entire family.

Janet is a middle-class White woman in her 40s who divorced when the children were 10 and 13. She works as a university professor in the field of special education. Janet recounts her experiences, describing Jake's teachers and her challenges in inclusion and in the delivery of services. She shares the emotions that arose in response to her relationships with various professionals and various life circumstances. Janet emphasizes the importance of teachers communicating to families that they care for their students with disabilities. She appears overwhelmed as her story leaves off, and we learn from Grace that Jake moves to join his sister and father in another state.

Grace, Jake's older sister, reflects on her experiences growing up. Now a 21-year-old college student, Grace's story provides a glimpse of her continuing attempt to make meaning of her family's challenges and the impact that "disability" has had and may continue to have on her. It is interesting to speculate how the experiences that Grace encountered have shaped her character. Grace's story demonstrates that a sibling's adaptation is a process, just as is a parent's adaptation.

JANET

Grace was 3 when Jake was born. She was playful but delicate, and she was such a joy that parenting did not seem all that hard. When Jake was a baby, we jokingly called him the bulldozer. He always knew what he wanted and would forge ahead, laying a path of destruction behind. As a toddler, he had beautiful curly blonde hair, and we let it grow until he was probably about 3. He was such a cute kid. Parenting was wonderful, but getting more challenging.

We first became concerned when, at age 2, Jake wasn't talking yet. He was also beginning to have temper tantrums that would continue forever. One time my husband had dropped me off with the kids for Grace's T-ball game. Halfway through the game, Jake threw a tantrum that was so long and intense that the other parents were getting more than a little annoyed. I didn't have a car, so I finally dragged him off kicking and screaming to an adjacent field until the game was over. Another mother, a complete stranger, came up to me after the game and suggested the name of a special program that dealt with children with behavior problems. I was embarrassed and annoyed at the stranger's suggestion. Her forwardness scared me too, I guess, because I had not considered that his temper tantrums were other than ordinary.

How did the diagnostician's priorities differ from Janet's priorities? From Janet's description, did the diagnostician's assessment employ a strength or deficit model?

I don't remember if it was before or after this incident, but we started by having his hearing tested. When his hearing tested normal, we took him to a private diagnostician who came highly recommended. She did some testing with Jake and interviewed me. Her report concluded that his language delay was due to a lack of appropriate educational experiences in the home. She cited numerous concepts that we had not attempted to teach, like color words or counting to 10—things that would have shown normal development on her tests. We were struggling to teach him words like mama and daddy, yes and no, milk, more—words that would help him communicate with us. She lectured me about the importance of a stimulating environment, and I don't think I have encountered such a condescending attitude in all the years since. I was outraged. She couldn't have a clue how rich his environment was. But even though I knew this intellectually, I felt this as a personal attack that triggered my already-present guilt. I was in graduate school and was working hard to juggle everything. It was obvious that we needed help, but there was no way that I was going to continue to take Jake to this lady for the language therapy she recommended.

I looked around more, and found a speech therapist at a hospital clinic, who I still think was one of the best teachers I've ever known. I took Jake to Mary twice a week. She had me watch their sessions so I would know what they were working on and how she did it. As they worked together, she made notes and recorded his progress, sharing this afterward and giving me ideas about carrying on the "work" in fun ways during the week. Even though I was trained in special education, seeing how effective her methods were with Jake was very helpful.

Early in Jake's work with Mary we had his hearing retested. We found that he had a significant hearing loss at moderate and high frequencies that the first evaluation missed. He was essentially not hearing any consonant sounds, and his language had developed consistent with what he heard. I had thought for some time that he had his own language that we just didn't understand. Now it made sense—he'd developed a vocabulary and syntax, but he was talking in vowel sounds. It must have been very frustrating for him. Once he got hearing aids and Mary taught him how to produce the new sounds he could hear, he made fast progress.

We also found an excellent preschool. I must have visited 10 programs before finding this one. It was perfect for Jake, as they provided the structured learning experiences that he needed, and they did it within a warm and creative play environment. They had developmental criteria for admission, and I remember vividly how I pondered over the application. I did not want to lie, but if I told them the whole truth, I didn't think they would admit him. I had done enough research to learn that preschools could be very selective. I tried to explain how wonderful he was—all the great stuff he could do. They accepted him. It is hard to express the depths of my gratitude—it's truly like trying to describe love. They were willing to take this kid who didn't talk, give him an incredibly rich environment, show him affection, and work through the temper tantrums he had when he didn't get what he wanted. Jake developed such a crush on his teacher that he invited her over to play with his toys and see his secret hiding place in the bushes. She was so sweet that she actually came. I still get emotional when I picture the two of them sitting in the dirt under the bushes playing together.

Jake had been in speech and preschool for a couple of years when my husband was offered a great job—only 1,100 mi away! It was a difficult decision. My husband and I had both grown up there, and we were very close to my family. Still, it really was a good time to move if we were ever going to; Jake was just ready to enter school, we had been considering changing schools for Grace, and I was just finishing graduate school. Scared stiff, we decided to do it.

> Census figures show that about one in six Americans move each year. The average American moves 11.7 times in a lifetime, and renters have much higher rates of moving than homeowners (Hansen, 2001)

We were leaving behind our family and friends, as well as Jake's preschool and speech. Jake had one little buddy at preschool that he was so tight with that you might wonder if they were joined at the hip. It was an emotional parting for all of us. I couldn't thank Jake's two programs enough. Jake had come a long way and was finally able to communicate with us verbally. His temper tantrums had pretty much disappeared. I loved these people like family.

GRACE

"Gracie, why are you moving?" my second-grade teacher asked. "My parents said that the schools in Maryland (pronounced Merry-land) are much better than they are here," I responded. I remember being all packed up and ready to go. I was still a bit peeved because in the packing my parents had thrown out the rubber rats in my pencil box. As I looked out the minivan window and waved good-bye to my grandparents, I knew I was going to miss them, but I did not realize how much.

Maryland was OK. I didn't mind the people at school and my teacher was pretty nice. The best thing about it, though, was that we had this huge backyard. Five acres of grass, woods, horse pasture, a creek, and even old houses we were not supposed to go into. It was the coolest thing a kid could ever imagine. Jake and I would come home from school and play all evening until we had to go in for dinner.

I became fast friends with two girls who had also moved there from other states. They were fun because they liked to get dirty like me. We would get into so much trouble we were eventually banned from seeing one another for awhile. One time my friend and I went into an old barn that was strictly forbidden and found some paint. We decided to paint the barn and then the inevitable paint fight started. That night each of us enjoyed a turpentine bath because it was oil-based paint we threw on each other.

JANET

It was a rough transition to Maryland. I had visited both schools the children would be going to before our move, and had sent reports and talked on the phone to the district administrator for hearing programs. I thought that we were all set to continue Jake's language program upon arrival. Instead, when we arrived and drove to the school to enroll, Grace was allowed to enroll, but not Jake. There was a little over a month of school left, and they said that he would have to wait until fall. Right off the bat, I had to fight with them to get him services. We compromised with speech therapy several days a week through the summer. Still, Jake wasn't around any children, and was so lonely that he cried every night for weeks for his friend back at the old preschool. It broke my heart.

In the fall, we enrolled Jake in two half-day kindergartens. He took an hour-long bus ride to the hearing-impaired program in the morning. Then, after the hour ride back, he attended the afternoon kindergarten at our neighborhood school. We lived close enough that there was no bus, but it was still some distance and there were no sidewalks. We cut a path through the waist-high weeds up the hill and placed rocks in the creek to make stepping-stones. I was working full-time, so I had to find baby-sitters to meet the kids after school. The first one was only a few years older than Grace, and she was often late, leaving Grace to help Jake down the hill and across the creek. It was a wonderful place for kids to grow up, though, and Grace and Jake played in the creek everyday catching salamanders and minnows.

Except for transportation and unreliable baby-sitters, this arrangement worked pretty well. Jake continued to make good progress. People could generally understand him once they got used to hearing him, he was no longer a behavior problem, and he was beginning to make friends. Eventually, we all got over the shock of leaving friends and family behind, and we each started to adapt.

That was also the year that we found out that Jake had inherited my muscular dystrophy. Not Duchenne's, which has such a terrible, certain outcome, but facioscapulahumeral dystrophy, which might or might not become seriously debilitating and life threatening. They couldn't tell us what would happen. I was devastated. Our pediatrician had picked it up during a routine school-entrance exam and sent us for a lengthy and difficult diagnostic process. One of the tests the doctor did required her to stick tiny pins into his muscles and move them around. It was a very uncomfortable test, and Jake was scared to death. I wanted to stay and hold him to calm him, but the doctor made me wait outside listening to him scream. Her philosophy toward it was "ignore the screaming and get it done," with no thought to discussing with a parent how it might be done in a way that wasn't so traumatizing. When I finally couldn't take it any longer, I broke into the room and told them that if I couldn't stay with him they would have to stop the test. I was much more cautious after that about being informed and preserving my trust bond with Jake, and less concerned with blindly following what well-intentioned adults decided would be best for us.

> Medical diagnosis often involves procedures that are uncomfortable and invasive. Janet is describing the electromyogram (EMG). In this test, small electrodes are placed in the muscle, allowing the doctor to measure the electrical impulses coming from the muscle. Other common tests for diagnosing muscular dystrophy include blood samples, a muscle biopsy, and a test of nerve conduction velocity in which electrical impulses are sent down the nerves of the arms and legs.

I was admittedly a mess. The Muscular Dystrophy Association clinic doctor revived a defunct parent-support group in honor of my crisis, and every month for several years this group provided me a major source of support. My husband accompanied me in the beginning, mostly because it was so emotionally draining for me to attend these meetings that I didn't feel like I could drive home safely. It's hard to describe the emotional state that I was in, but I cried when I tried to talk, when another parent cried, in other words, just about all the time. It was really an altered state, and I could see that many of the other parents were sharing this same space. There was baby-sitting provided, but I did not want to take the kids because I did not want to have to explain to them why I could not quit crying. As time went on, I could see that I was less needy and emotionally fragile. I even recognized that new parents who were joining us were as fragile as I had once been. It was reassuring to recognize that I was moving to a better place.

GRACE

In growing up, I always had an excuse. "Oh well, my mom or my brother has this horrible disease, see, so I get depressed sometimes and that's why I can't..." I would pull it out on days when I was feeling particularly bad. It was always something to fall back on. If I was feeling depressed for no particular reason, I'd just decide that I was depressed because I was worried about the quality of Jake's life. I also would tell other people about it if I needed them to be kind to me. I used it the way many people use it all the time. It was the thing that made me different.

For a long time I would say things that weren't really true about my home situation. I would give people the impression that I dwelled on my brother or my mother's disability more than I really did. I always felt bad about this, but then reasoned that if I needed a good reason to be depressed, that was one. I would convince myself that I really did feel bad about it; that I wasn't lying. The truth is, yes, I did think about my brother's life a lot more than most 10-year-olds. I did cry when I thought about things that people said about him or the way people stared everywhere we went. It was an issue in my life. But I think that using it as an excuse to be depressed was the wrong way to go. It did not bother me that much yet. It was just a factor in my life.

Some local disability organizations sponsor sibling support groups. The Sibling Support Project at http://www.thearc.org/siblingsupport may help you to locate a group in your area. This national program maintains a database of programs for brothers and sisters of people with special needs, conducts educational workshops on sibling issues, trains adults to provide sibshops for children, sponsors listservs for children, and disseminates awareness materials.

JANET

When it was time to plan Jake's move to first grade, the district recommended full-time placement in the hearing-impaired program. Jake had done fine in our neighborhood kindergarten, however, so I didn't see any reason to bus him an hour away. He was pretty much on level with the other kids in his class. We had put a lot of effort into helping him establish friends that he played with after school. He was happy, he was learning, and his language was developing better through his play after school. What more could a mom want? After we refused the hearing-impaired program, the district switched to recommending the physical disabilities program that was also across town. They said that it would be better for Jake because he would get more attention, and they kept insisting that

I just go visit. I never doubted that Jake would get more teacher attention in a special education program, but this was just a straight clash of values. I wanted him to have kids to play with, and to be a part of the neighborhood. His program across town had actually interfered with that. I never did visit the physical disabilities program. After numerous meetings at the central administration building and countless phone calls, they agreed to let him attend first grade at our neighborhood school.

I don't know if it was "payback" or just trying to prove a point, but in first grade we got our all-time worst teacher. Mrs. Stepford had decided before she ever met Jake that he should not be at this school, and certainly not in her class. She was nasty from our first conversation. She was always precise, cold, demanding, and negative. I always felt on the defensive. Every statement she made was calculated to document why Jake should not be in her class. To prove her point, she required Jake to complete all assignments that the class did while he was in pull-out services, sending it home as homework when there wasn't time at school. She wrote everything down, dated it, and asked us to sign that we had read it. She never commented on anything he could do or had learned—only what he could not do. Her first progress report said

> Jake has made little progress in reading this quarter. Jake is easily distracted and does not attend in small- or large-group settings. Jake is inconsistent in returning homework and is disorganized even with a structured routine. Many of Jake's homework assignments or incomplete daily assignments were not returned this quarter.

I grew to hate her. I was so proud of all the progress he had made, and all she could see was what he could not do. I believe that she was threatened by any little success that he had, because she had been so adamant that he would not be able to keep up. If he did, she would lose face. I know that part of it was that she was concerned that he would be hurt, because he was already falling sometimes. But instead of helping him deal with it and live as normal a life as possible, she just wanted somebody else to deal with it.

We must have had a zillion meetings that year to "review his progress." But each meeting's purpose was really to say to us that he was making insufficient progress and should be placed somewhere else—anywhere else. One meeting was to discuss the teacher's concern that he was socially isolated (and would be better off with other hearing-impaired kids). I was already becoming creative in trying to help him develop playmates among some of the boys, but it was not easy because most of them played team sports together and were already forming cliques. Then, at another time, the principal called us to a meeting because Jake and several other boys had gotten into mischief on the playground. While I nodded solemnly and agreed to the punishment, I silently celebrated that he was included in the troublemaking!

That year was one of the worst of my life. At the same time I was fighting with the school, I could see Jake losing strength. He tired easily and was falling more and more. The disease progressed so fast that I didn't see how he could possibly live to graduate from high school. That rearranges your priorities! I became fanatical about packing all the normal childhood experiences into what might be a short life. We took family outings every weekend, went to Disneyland, and took walks in our woods each evening. We traveled to the many historical sites around us, prompting a future teacher to remark that he'd never met a child with such a good understanding of history. Jake had to stop every few minutes and find a bench to rest on, so my husband carried him on his shoulders much of the time. I don't know how to explain the emotional resistance to buying a wheelchair, but it was a huge step when we finally broke down and bought one. Meanwhile, we received piles of Xeroxed worksheets each night, which we helped Jake complete if we had time; but play and family time clearly took priority.

I made considered risks to allow Jake to lead as normal a life as possible. I remember all the times he would ask me to lift him to the bottom limbs of the tree that Grace and the other children climbed. It made me a wreck to watch, so I had to busy myself reading or pulling weeds. With the teacher continually saying that Jake could not do this and that, I took the same approach to risk-taking at school. Inside, I was petrified, but outside I believed that I had to present myself as a confident advocate—a mother who was absolutely certain that Jake would succeed at whatever he attempted. A lot of times, I really was confident that he could do whatever it was. Sometimes, I knew for a fact I was bluffing, maybe he could, maybe he couldn't. But I couldn't let anyone see the fear. I knew that he would not learn what he did not try.

> Do you think Janet's perceived need not to show her true fears was justified? Why or why not? What was Janet afraid of?

Looking back on that time, I am resentful that I had such a fight on the school front while dealing with the emotional impact of Jake's disease. Instead of receiving encouragement and support from the professionals around me, I could never admit a fear or worry. I spent a lot of nights crying myself to sleep. But the people at Jake's school never saw any of this. I was certain they would have seen it as weakness and pounced on the occasion to get rid of him, just as they documented every other weakness.

We fought all year long. The school finally accepted that there was no defensible reason why Jake should not be allowed to return again the next year. I still remember one of the very few positive interactions we had with any educators that year. The school psychologist said in a meeting that she admired what we had done for Jake that year. Even though her support was late coming, it seemed sincere and I appreciated it.

GRACE

It was not until I entered college that I began to focus on Jake's disease as much as I do. It has been hell to watch its progression. I think getting older made me put into focus the reality of my brother's life and my mother's future. I began to realize how tough growing up disabled had to be and felt guilty because I am not disabled. It scares me in a way I cannot describe. When I was younger, I would have terrifying nightmares of things getting bigger. There would be bags of gold or piles of corn. The piles or bags would just get bigger and bigger, and I would scream and scream and wake up crying. Jake's muscular dystrophy feels much the same to me. It is out of my control, and that scares me. I feel helpless; there is nothing I can do but watch. And pray.

The more I thought about my brother, the more I began not telling people about him. Not because I didn't want people to know, but because I didn't want their pity anymore. I don't need it. I was sure my brother didn't need it. It became something real to me, not just a story to tell. I find myself not mentioning Jake's or my mom's disability to people very often these days. I have come to the conclusion that I did have a lot of things happen and circumstances that could be considered reason to be a messed up kid, but I came out OK. The past couple of years I have become someone I can be proud of as far as how I deal with having disability in my family.

JANET

Immediately after Mrs. Stepford, our "worst-ever" teacher, came Mrs. Beckley, perhaps the "best-ever" teacher. When Mrs. Beckley learned that she was to have Jake in her second grade, she immediately told us that she knew it would be a great year. She said she was delighted to have Jake in her class and she knew that he would do fine. This was such a gift. It said that we could stop fighting—watching our backsides—and actually trust that someone would care about Jake again. She used to have class plays and choral readings to which parents were invited. Jake always had a part; well, not just "a" part, but he was just as important a part of the class as any other child there. His father and I were always there, so proud of his achievements. She was so loving with the children. His first report card started, "Jake is a great boy to have in our class and a source of inspiration to me. He has good spirit and tries hard." She went on to tell us specifics about what he could do, and what we needed to work on. I still have a picture of she and Jake hanging in my office. Jake is in his Superman costume, and Mrs. Beckley is the witch who is pushing his wheelchair in the Halloween parade.

According to Knapp and Turnbull (1990), the conventional wisdom that students must master basic skills before progressing to higher order skills has been found to be a barrier to many students. Such a linear model of curriculum organization tends to underestimate what students are capable of and postpones more interesting and challenging work while students are exposed repeatedly to an impoverished "basics" curriculum. This has the unintended effect of placing a ceiling on their learning.

Having Mrs. Beckley also meant, much to the district's discomfort, that we could focus again on Grace's needs, which had taken a backseat to Jake's. She had always had a lot of trouble with spelling and math facts, and I had had occasional run-ins with teachers who wanted to track her in lower groups until she "caught up." She didn't need to be held back; on the contrary, she needed more meaningful challenges. In second grade, her teacher thought I was crazy when I insisted that they move her forward two ability groupings rather than backward. She couldn't tell you what 8 plus 5 was without counting, but if you let her use her fingers, she could solve very advanced story problems. The more her teachers held her back to work on flash cards and worksheets, the more bored she became with school.

Now that we didn't have a list of "to do's" concerning Jake, there was time that we could meet with Grace's teacher, give her extra help, etcetera. We ended up having her tested for learning disabilities both at school and privately. Eventually filing for a due process hearing and going to mediation, we reached a settlement. The school provided her an extra level of support and made some accommodations, but they did not label her as learning disabled. I was fine with that, as long as she received the help she needed.

GRACE

I have gained many things from having a sibling with a disability. I don't say the word "retard." I never have. I have struggled most of my life to make sure I knew the correct terms for everything. I think this is because I know that there are people behind these labels. Jake was never retarded. One reason I hate that word so much, though, is because its common misuse illustrates how many people don't understand that every disabled person is not "mentally challenged."

I notice people in wheelchairs—as in I can hear a motorized wheelchair from miles away and probably have a pretty good idea what kind it is. If I'm in a room with someone in a wheelchair, I notice it. I know what they are doing, and I try to know how they are feeling just by observation. This is a sort of research. What does Jake go through? This is one way for me to find out.

There is a guy at my school. Let's call him George. George has cerebral palsy. He has been at school as long as I've been here. George has long hair he keeps in a ponytail, a good sense of humor, a shy demeanor, and listens to some pretty good music. I have done some top-secret investigating and have also found out that he is an art major. He paints with his mouth. George does not know this, but he is my brother. I have turned him into Jake. And so as long as I've been at school, I've wanted to talk to George. Just say hi, I keep telling myself.

> A number of etiquette guides have been developed for interacting with individuals with disabilities. Several helpful guides are available on the United Cerebral Palsy Web site at http://www.ucpa.org.

One day I was approaching an intersection. I saw George jerking around in his chair at the crosswalk. I knew that the light at this particular intersection does not turn for a very long time. I began to get excited, now was my chance to say hi. It would not be out of the blue, because we were both stuck at this intersection. Then the dread set in. What if I said something stupid, or if he wanted to say hi back and got nervous and began to jerk and could not talk back. What then? I found my pace beginning to slow. I forced myself back to the original pace. Just as I started my internal pep talk again, George turned and went down the road. I breathed a sigh of relief.

I thought about this near encounter for a long time. I knew I was disappointed, but I didn't know it was with myself. I told myself it wasn't my fault he had decided to go another way. It wasn't. My sigh of relief was what was really bothering me. It began to hit me. I had done to George what has been done to my brother countless times. Wasn't I supposed to be better, or at least better educated than that? I talked to my brother about this. I wanted his advice on how to be smooth when approaching people with disabilities. We talked about the right and wrong things to say. Example: "Hey, what's wrong with you?"—wrong. "Hey, what's up?"—right. I laughed. I knew that. We joked around about the Bible-thumping ladies that come up to Jake and tell him they will pray for him. I always want to punch them in the face!

JANET

I eventually developed a pretty good relationship with many of the professionals in each district. Of course, there were many "fools" to be suffered as well. One high-level bureaucrat caused us quite a bit of grief getting anything accomplished. Over the years, she had developed her own way of doing things to make her life easier, and deviations from those ways were difficult for her. She was one, too, who lumped together all kids with the same classification—as if you could read the label and know the kid. I remember her trying to explain to me in one IEP meeting why Jake needed a vocabulary goal. The testing indicated that he was at the 85th percentile in vocabulary. I was happy with that and thought he had a great vocabulary. I wanted them to drop the goal and move on to work on something else; he had plenty of other speech and language problems. She said that all hearing-impaired kids need help with vocabulary, and their goal was to bring him up to the 100th percentile. I realized she didn't know what percentile meant. It was hard to have respect for an administrator who was so sure of herself that she would not listen to a parent and yet was so ignorant. Not to mention how hard it makes it then to trust that she knows anything else about my particular child's needs.

There are many stories—the teacher who expressed her caring for the students by smothering and over-protecting them, the paraprofessionals that were expected to tend to Jake's needs all day long at the table in the back of the classroom so the teacher could attend to "her" students, and the unending stream of papers that Jake brought home each night for my signature as proof that I'd done what I was asked. There was the physical education teacher who called me the first day of school to say he was new to the school, that he was glad that Jake would be in one of his classes, and that he wanted to do some reading about muscular dystrophy if I had anything to recommend. And the principal who reassured me in our first meeting that whatever came up, we could deal with it together. His wife used a wheelchair like Jake did by that point, and he said he knew there would be some problems we'd have to work out, but we would. And the principal who found a couple of kids to be pen pals with my kids when we were going to move there. And the case manager who used to meet with me before IEP meetings to plan "our" strategies, outline arguments, or draft goals. I could go on and on.

GRACE

After my parents divorced, I moved to Texas with Mom and Jake. I was 15 years old at the time. Because my mom is also disabled, I ended up doing a lot more around the house than the typical 15-year-old. I understood why, but still felt angry about it. I wanted to be a normal kid. My resentment grew, and my mom and I started fighting more and more. I finally had to move. I moved back East to live with my dad.

After about 2 months there, I realized I began to feel a horrible guilt. How were Mom and Jake going to get on without me? I never completely got rid of the guilt that went along with leaving Jake and mom. I would not go to sleep at night because I was worrying that he might die and I'd not know until the next day. I couldn't bear the idea of not being there.

My worst fear is that my brother, Jake, will die before I do. This fear has manifested itself such that I can successfully manage to ignore it for months at a time, but whenever anything goes wrong, it is the first thing I cry about.

JANET

Our latest challenge was getting physical therapy at school. Not one child at the high school receives PT, including a class for students with physical disabilities that draws across the district! PT was on Jake's IEP in middle school, and he was supposed to be getting it all along. But the district never hired a therapist to cover the high school, and when he moved up from middle school, the therapy never got started. I complained, so they reevaluated him and said that PT was no longer educationally necessary. The regulations say that the therapy must be educationally necessary, not just medically necessary. Therefore, the district's standard response is that therapy is necessary for medical reasons. It's then up to the parent to make a convincing argument that the therapy is relevant and necessary for the child's education. Of course, most parents aren't able to do that because it is a word game, and they aren't given the rules. Doctors' reports or recommendations don't usually help much, and may even hurt, because of course, they use medical language and point out medical needs. Most doctors don't know much about teaching and haven't really thought about what it takes to educate a child. Eventually, Jake had back surgery and did have additional medical needs, so it became even harder to fight.

One of my major complaints with so many administrators we have dealt with is that their strategy was just to wear you down. They didn't return my phone calls, so I had to call and call trying to find people at their desks. If they did call, they said that they'd check into the problem and get back to me, which they never did. Maybe, eventually, they would say that they were going to provide whatever service starting in 2 weeks, and it never would. Finally, it would be spring and they would say, "It's too late in the year to start now." Then I'd be forced to begin the process all over again the next school year when I noticed that the service still wasn't being provided. I'm not exaggerating. I've been working on getting PT for a year and a half. A parent has to practically devote full-time to making phone calls, letter writing, or going to meetings. Then you need to document each of your efforts and check to see that the district did what it said it would. It's absolutely exhausting. When you have a child with physical problems, you have to multiply this by all the doctors, therapists, and social service agencies that also aren't in and tell you to call back later. I am a person who operates with lists, and one time I was sitting at work making calls most of the morning when I realized that I'd made phone calls or had appointments about Jake almost every day for months. By this time, I was a single mom, trying to work full-time, and the calls and appointments were wearing me down.

> Do you return telephone calls promptly? Do you have a system for monitoring case follow-up?

While we were arguing about whether PT was necessary for educational or medical reasons, Jake was still sitting in a wheelchair all day, muscles atrophying, contractures forming, and pressure sores developing. My medical insurance would not pay for therapy.

> Would teachers help parents more if they could? What demands are competing with the family's needs?

Jake was growing increasingly depressed because his physical condition was worsening, and he felt helpless. He didn't want to go anywhere or do anything, and would only say that it was all a waste of time. He was flunking most of his subjects because he wouldn't do homework. I made him go to counseling, but getting him there was a major battle each time. I not only had to take off work, but then I'd have to argue with him about whether he should go. I understand only too well why parents give up. The nightmare is coming back with my retelling. There were times that I just didn't know how much longer I could hold it together. I was begging for help, watching my child suffer emotionally, and every door I knocked on was slammed in my face.

This kind of a situation is so very painful for a parent that I wish I could express it better. If you really understood the pain that is there sometimes, you would be careful not to add to it. I really want to believe that teachers and administrators are caring and compassionate people. That's why they went into the profession to begin with, isn't it?

GRACE

It's Mom, Jake, and I on a horse drawn buggy. We are riding through the woods to get home. I am sitting in front of Jake holding his front up. The buggy is very bumpy; we are going over all sorts of roots and rocks. I am quite nervous about the rod in Jake's back. I am picturing it ripping through his skin. I am becoming more and more frantic as Jake's pain becomes more and more evident. His face is brave; he is trying to keep his lips together. I really want to get home so this nightmare will end. The driver gets a call on his cellular phone. He stops the buggy. He hangs up and says to us, "Well, looks like we're going to have to stop here and wait for the horses to come, and you'll have to do the rest of the trip on horseback." Anger and hysteria overwhelm me and I say, trying to sound calm, "I don't think that is a possibility, we need to get home." Just at that point, Jake screams or moans. I turn my head to see him throw up. His face is of excruciating pain and his neck is red and stained. I wake up.

> Grace's fear illustrates Meyer's (1993) point that a major need for siblings is accurate information about the disability. The surgical procedure Grace describes is a spinal fusion. The surgery stabilizes the spinal column by fusing the vertebrae together with bone grafts and/or metal rods. After a recuperation of gradually increasing activity levels, the individual can typically resume an active life without concern.

The first time I really heard my brother screaming in pain was after his back surgery. He had a metal rod fused into his back. The screams and moans were almost constant. I visited right after the surgery had been done. I thought because my grandparents were there visiting, this was the perfect time to go. I was wrong. My nightmares are now more audibly accurate.

This metal rod has become sort of an obsession of mine. I think about it whenever we fly anywhere and they are transferring him from one seat to another. I am so worried that they will move him wrong and that rod will poke some internal thing that shouldn't be poked, or my worst fear, that it will actually rip out his neck.

JANET

We have had some of the best teachers in the world and some of the worst, and plenty in between. When you're the best you are going to have my undying loyalty, perhaps love. When you're the worst you are going to have a huge pain in the neck, perhaps a due process hearing. If you are one of the best, I'd like for you to understand that my best, for awhile, is going to be vigilance. My trust will be gained slowly, as I see that you follow through on what you say you will do. I need to see that you are aware of what Jake needs and will try to find ways to provide that, and that you will not sacrifice his needs to your schedule or the way you have always done things. When I begin to trust you, I will relax my vigilance for a much-needed respite. That may appear to you as a lack of support or involvement. I am probably just attending to something else that has been neglected too long.

I really want to work with you. It is so much easier, and I like it when you also like me. I do care what you think, but I care even more about my kid's education. I have to do whatever it takes to get his needs met. Sometimes it seems that the only way to do that is to confront you or complain to someone else. I wish that I could always do that in the best possible manner, but sometimes my emotions are so heightened that I just can't do it any better than what you see. It's just because I believe that what you do is so important and I care so much.

GRACE

I don't really know how sisters treat brothers without muscular dystrophy. I always thought we were pretty average. We joke around with each other, and I give him a hard time about anything and everything. He returns the favor. I have come to realize over the years, though, that I am more protective of my brother than are most sisters. For some reason, I have taken on the role of MOM when I am with Jake. I don't think that is helpful to either him or my family.

Take last week for example. I came home from college to spend a relaxing couple of days with my friends. One morning I was getting up early to go to a museum downtown. When I woke up, I was disappointed to see that the sky was gray and it was going to be a cold day to walk around outside. Jake moved back to dad's house awhile back, so I went upstairs to check on Jake. The first thing he said to me was that he needed me to check the ramp to see how icy it was. The ramp was bad enough that I almost slipped when I first stepped on it. I told Jake that I didn't think it was safe for him to go out onto the ramp. His chair would surely slide out of control. He was upset because he had an important assignment due that day. I began to stress-out. What was I going to do? I didn't know how to help him without giving up my plans. About 1 1/2 hr later, Jake had worked it out on his own, and I had messed up the day for me and my friends. I felt angry that I had taken it upon myself to try and "fix" the difficult situation that Jake was in. It wasn't my responsibility to fix it, and in the end, he solved the problem himself. Jake is 18 years old. He is not a baby that needs me to take care of him. His problems are complicated by his disability, but that does not mean that I should try to solve all his problems.

I met someone once that had seen a piece of theater I wrote and performed about having a brother with a disability. He said that he had seen my show and that he understood what I was going through. I was excited because usually when I meet siblings or family members of a disabled person there is some sort of understanding that I don't often find in people that do not have relatives with disabilities. The fact was, he didn't have any relatives with disabilities, but he had a friend whose brother was disabled. He went on to say that his friend had always resented his brother because of the special treatment he got. He talked of how his friend was always complaining that his little brother got all the attention and that all the money was always spent on him and his medical expenses. I didn't really know what to say. I felt horrible that someone could resent his brother because of something that was not his fault. Not that I didn't understand how it could happen. From what I hear, it happens all of the time. I just can't relate though. I am always willing to take Jake places or to get him things. Whatever he needs, or wants, I am willing and most of the time, pleased to do. I think I'm fortunate enough to have parents that raised me not to know what sort of special treatment Jake was getting. I've never resented Jake. As far as I was concerned, Jake was just my little brother.

Although I have written only about Jake and his disability, this is not what has impacted me most about having Jake as a brother. Jake has been my best friend for as long as I can remember. Jake has mad artist skills, a crazy sense of humor, and he doesn't take things for granted. He is aware of things that other people overlook. He has a pure heart and soul, and I've never seen Jake be mean. I'm not saying he's perfect, but his problems are not ones with his heart or soul. Knowing Jake has given me something to aspire to become. I only wish everyone could see what I see in him.

Activities

1. Compile two lists: (a) list everything that teachers or administrators did that Janet would consider best practices and (b) list everything that teachers or administrators did that Janet would consider bad practice.

2. Conduct research to locate support groups in your community for parents or siblings of children with disabilities. Call various disability organizations and locate at least three parent or sibling support groups that meet regularly. Develop a list that includes the group name, the contact person's name and telephone number, the frequency and location of their meetings, and a brief description of what occurs at their meetings.

3. *Discuss:* What are Janet's values? What experiences or beliefs are influential in the way Janet approaches problems? What past experiences and values do you have that might cause your perspective to differ from Janet's perspective? Are you aware of theory or research that informs your perspective?

4. Janet did not elaborate on the district's possible reasons for recommending placement in a class for students who are physically disabled. Make a list of the reasons that the district might have considered this the placement of choice. Then, briefly discuss the values represented by the district's recommendation and how these values compare to those that Janet discusses.

5. Test results may use both percentiles and percentages. If Jake's vocabulary was at the 85th percentile, his scores were better than 85% of the children tested at his age. The administrator appears to have misinterpreted his test results, assuming that he had answered 85% of the questions correctly. Role-play the IEP meeting in which a teacher must explain the test results to Janet, and then facilitate the development of goals.

6. Conduct research about the ways in which guardianship is determined upon the death of the parents of a child with disabilities. In your report, discuss the factors that would influence whether a sibling should assume guardianship.

7. *Discuss:* Hearing impairments in very young children sometimes go undetected because of the difficulty in testing these children. Given that different sounds are produced at different frequencies, discuss how a hearing loss at various frequencies might affect receptive language and speech. Relate this to Jake's acquisition of language, referring to a picture of the "speech banana." If you are able to obtain access to copies of different audiograms showing hearing losses, speculate about the heard or missed speech sounds.

8. In small groups, visit a children's bookstore or conduct an Internet search to find a book for children who have a brother or sister with disabilities. Read the book to the class and provide a group commentary on the information and subtext that the book conveys to children.

9. *Discuss:* Grace mentions her mother's disability, but Janet does not. What are some possible reasons that Janet did not discuss her own disability. Was it irrelevant to Janet, was she embarrassed or ashamed by it, or was there some other reason for Janet not mentioning her disability?

10. Interview the adult brother or sister of a person with disabilities. Ask them to discuss if they sometimes felt neglected or jealous of their sibling and if they believe that they had a different relationship with their sibling than their schoolmates had with their siblings. In addition, ask them to discuss if they believe that their family benefited in ways that families without disabilities do not. Determine if they currently assist in their sibling's care and if they expect to be involved in their sibling's care in the future.

11. Interview the parent of a child with special medical needs. Ask them to discuss the approximate number of telephone calls they have made to professionals (educators, counselors, therapists, doctors, advocacy groups, social service agencies, etc.) during the current week and how much time would they estimate was spent in those telephone calls. Did they have trouble reaching the professionals that they tried to contact by telephone, and were the messages they left returned in an acceptable time frame? In addition, ask them to discuss how often they take their child to various appointments and if they missed work to do this? Are their employers supportive and flexible about this need? If they have other children in the home at this time, what arrangements do they make for their care?

12. We did not hear from Jake's father in this story—his perspective of the issues, what his needs were, and so forth. Conduct research on the issues and the needs that fathers' confront and the organizations that provide support and information specifically to fathers. Report these issues to the class and note the services offered locally and nationally.

13. Janet reports feeling overwhelmed by her inability to obtain physical therapy for Jake and to deal effectively with his depression. Conduct research to find resources or programs in your state or local area that could provide helpful services.

14. Janet quotes several passages from progress reports to show the teachers' attitudes toward Jake. As Grace's teacher, develop a note for the comment section of

Grace's progress report, including both strengths and areas that need improvement. In small groups, read your comments and discuss the teacher attitudes conveyed by each progress report.

15. *Discuss:* How typical is Grace's anxiety about approaching the college student
    who uses a wheelchair? Do you think that it is more difficult for individuals with
    disabilities to make friends? What strategies have you learned for helping stu-
    dents with disabilities integrate socially?

16. Describe the best practices that teachers and other helping professionals should
    use to assist this family.

17. Write an analysis of this case, drawing parallels from this case to (a) your own
    experiences; (b) theory and research from class discussions, course readings, and
    knowledge gained in previous classes; and (c) other cases in this book.

Suggested Resources

Center for Mental Health in Schools. (1997). Welcoming strategies for newly arrived students and their families. *Addressing Barriers to Learning, 2*(4). Los Angeles: School
Mental Health Project—UCLA. Available for download at smhp.psych.ucla.edu

Cramer, S., Erzkus, A., Pope, K., Roeder, J., Tone, T., & Mayweather, K. (1997). Con-
necting with siblings. *Teaching Exceptional Children, 30*(1), 46–51.

Jameson, E. J. (1999). Managed care and children with chronic illnesses or disabilities.
Exceptional Parent; 29(9), 104-8. Available for download at
www.eparent.com/healthcare/chronic.htm

Meyer, D., & Vadas, P. (1994). *Sibshops: Workshops for siblings of children with special
needs*. Baltimore: Paul H. Brookes.

Meyer, D., Vadas, P., & Fewell, R. R. (1996). *Living with a brother or sister with special
needs: A book for sibs* (2nd ed.). Seattle: University of Washington Press.

Powell, T., & Gallagher, P. (1993). *Brothers and sisters: A special part of exceptional
families*. Baltimore: Paul H. Brookes.

Online Resources

Visit the Family Voices Web site at www.familyvoices.org for information and resources
concerning the health care of children with special health needs.

References

Hansen, K. A. (2001). *Geographical mobility*. U.S. Census Bureau, Population Division.
Retrieved May 18, 2003, from www.census.gov/population/www/pop-profile/geomob.html

Knapp, M. S., & Turnbull, B. J. (1990). *Better schooling for the children of poverty— Alternatives to conventional wisdom. Vol. 1. Summary.* Washington, DC: U.S. Department of Education, Office of Planning Budget and Evaluation.

Meyer, D. (1993, May). Siblings of children with special health and developmental needs: Programs, services, and considerations. *ARCH National Resource Center for Respite and Crisis Care Services Fact Sheet, 23*. Retrieved June 14, 2001, from www.chtop.com/archfs23.htm.

CHAPTER TWELVE

I Love My Baby:
Rita's Story

Commentary: Rita's son, Jacob, was born with a severely underdeveloped brain, a condition that almost always results in death within a few days or weeks. Still, the hospital released Rita and Jacob the next morning and did not provide the necessary information and training to deal with her son's needs or the psychological preparation or support to address this family crisis. Unwilling to do nothing and watch her baby die, Rita begins a struggle that takes her to this place 5 years later.

This case provides an opportunity to reflect upon and discuss the genesis of such care. Was this particular medical staff unaware of Rita's needs or how to help? Is this representative of a disparity in basic medical care provided to African Americans, or women, or those with a particular type of insurance? Was there an assumption because of Rita's educational or economic level, appearance, or manner of speech that this mother would not understand explanations of medical conditions and procedures? Rita's use of nonstandard grammar and informal, simple sentence structure in this story will cause you to grapple with these questions and perhaps your own prejudices. What assumptions are you making, and what attitudes are conveyed to others as you discuss how to assist Rita's family?

A sense of strength, commitment, and determination is captured from this single mother of three who is in her late 30s and belongs to a support group of African American women who meet monthly. Rita's determination to care for her child will call on you to evaluate your reactions to her decisions and how your values might influence your ideas for assisting Rita. While Rita's problems appear far removed from school concerns in many regards, early interventionists understand that their role on the professional team begins at birth and extends far beyond one specific family member and traditional school issues.

NOTES ON A NAPKIN

When I was pregnant 3 months I asked for an amniocentesis because I was high risk at my age and I had problem with my thyroids. But the problems had been corrected and he said I didn't need it. Now this doctor decided to go into practice for himself, and I changed doctors about 8 months.

This new doctor wanted to start over with a fresh sonogram. That is when he saw there was something wrong. I just had finished the sonogram. I was told that my baby's head was small. But that was it. I went to the head office of OB/GYN. The director was not in, so I spoke with the head nurse. Her and my friend that was with me went into this board

Amniocentesis can test for several medical conditions, including chromosome abnormalities, infection, and neural tube defects. Amniotic fluid is extracted through a slender needle that is inserted into the woman's abdomen.

room. My friend sat at a desk and got a napkin and start taking notes on the questions that I was asking. The information that she was writing was going to affect me the rest of my life and she was writing on a napkin! I told her that was all right.

I told the nurse I demand to talk with the doctor. I need to know the outcome of my baby. He came out and told me that we would just have to pray. I left. During the time I was watching the news, it told about some babies born without completely developed brains in Louisiana. I hoped that wouldn't be the case with me. It seems that every time I would always be at the right place at the right time when the story of the babies would come on. I said later, after Jacob was born, it was God's way of letting me know what was going to happen.

MY HOSPITAL STAY

I went the full 9 months, no problem. I had a baby boy name Jacob, weight 7 lb, 6 oz. My OB handed me my baby. He looked small all over. It was hard for me to tell if something was wrong. The baby was delivered vaginally, which I thought was weird because they said something might be wrong with his head. Why not do a C-section? I didn't think about asking until later. The baby cried and they suctioned. They gave oxygen immediately, he was dried off and was crying. They gave him to me and then finish up.

I was in a room with another lady that just had her baby. I waited. No one came with my baby. She had company all that night. But I was still waiting. The social worker came by as she was leaving for home. She had that look on her face like she wanted to tell me something. But I told her that I had not spoke with my OB doctor yet. So whatever she had to say would have to wait. The evening pass and I still had not seen my baby. The doctor came in about 6:30–7:00 p.m. and say we are still running tests. So about 10:00 p.m. I ask what was going on. They told me that they were trying to feed the baby but it went poorly. So I drank some coffee and asked if I could go and try to feed him. So I did, out of a 2-oz bottle. I ask the nurse for something to help me sleep, because it was 12:00 a.m. before I went to bed.

Hospital stays for delivery have grown shorter and shorter in recent decades, with many insurance companies pushing women into having what became known as *drive-through deliveries*. PL 104-204, signed into law by President Clinton in 1996, assured mothers and newborns hospital stays of up to 48 hr after a normal delivery (Holland Sentinel, 1999).

Then the next day someone woke me up and said it was time for me to get up, that I was being release from the hospital. I told them that I was tired. I asked about Jacob. They told me that he was still being seen by the doctor. A neurological doctor came in to see me. He seem like he didn't know what to say. He said "The baby might have seizures, but don't stick anything in his mouth." He told me the location of his office, and that was it. No one still say nothing on what was wrong with my baby. My doctor came in and told me that the baby was OK. But he had a look on his face as if "she still doesn't know." So I get released. I thought that I was going to be here for awhile because of Jacob's problem.

I FOUGHT HARD

We go home, and before 12:00 p.m. the baby starts having seizures. I call the HMO and they tell me to bring him to the emergency room. The doctor that was on call was mad. He ask "You mean to tell me no one told you what was wrong with the baby?" I said "Yes, no one told me." He sat down with me and told me that Jacob has to take seizure medicine the rest of his life, and what Jacob had was microcephaly and anencephaly. Later what was going though my head was that I should not had Jacob vaginally—it should have been C-section, and they thought that he was going to die, so that why it was so bad for me at first.

According to Schaefer (1995), more than half of the infants born with anencephaly are stillborn and 90% die within 1 week; the infant rarely lives for more than 1 month. For hospice services, an individual must have a limited life expectancy, usually defined as up to 6 months, and must no longer be seeking or receiving curative treatments to be eligible. A do not resuscitate (DNR) order may be expected but cannot be required (National Hospice Foundation, 2000).

Anyway I'd taken him home and he wouldn't eat or drink regular baby milk. So I tried goat milk and all kinds of milk. So I start with Carnation milk for babies. Then trying to find a different kind of nipple he would suck. So we start out with a 2-oz bottle. So I went to the store and got some olive oil. I soak my front door and soak Jacob's head and prayed over him. I ask God to save my baby and to keep him alive. We still saw new reports about the babies but not so often. I tried to breast-feed, but I was still upset about what was going on. For 2 months I was still having feeding problems.

I would talk with the doctor about Jacob losing oxygen. She act like she did not know what I talk about. He would have congestion real bad, and they didn't want to give medicine. But I went into the HMO office so much they gave me some.

Then about 6 or 7 months Jacob received hospice, which was good. She got a nurse chaplain and social worker to come out. It's funny, they were trying to help me get ready for death. And I wasn't ready for that. So I still fought hard. The doctor kept telling me not to call 911, to call hospice if something happen to Jacob. I couldn't do that. But every time she told me that, my heart would break. Because I love him and I didn't want anything to happen to him.

BACK TO WORK

It was time for me to, I guess, play like I was going back to work. I wasn't ready. I just was hit with having a child who would be disabled. I didn't know if I could face my coworker. Everyone expect for people to be OK and sometime it's not. Anyway, my boss was giving me a hard time about coming back to work. I told him I need more time, that my baby was sick. So I had extra time.

Then when it was time, I had to find a day care or someone to keep Jacob and know how to deal with his need one-on-one. I found a place so Jacob and his older brother would attend. Jacob would drink 2 oz, three times a day and two bottles at home. Then juice and some water. I later got my own suction machine for Jacob because let me tell you about the time that Jacob got sick at the day care and they call me. I was closer to the hospital so I tell them I would meet them there. Since they left before I did, I thought they would be already inside checking in. I got there and got so upset thinking all kind of things, so I go running down the hall and here they come just getting there. They could not get the phlegm out of his throat, and so came in cause it was choking him.

> According to Blaska (1998), parents report that watching other people's children reach developmental milestones may produce a new period of grief and a subsequent adjustment process.

So I called my job and told them that everything was all right. Another girl had a baby right after I did. She would always ask me if my baby was walking or sitting up. I told her that he was disabled. She still would ask, so one day she ask me about his size, and I told her that just because I don't cry all the time in front of her didn't mean I didn't hurt. She said I didn't act like anything was wrong.

The social worker for hospice was really nice. But the nurse, she could not understand what I was doing. Jacob had hospice for 365 days, and right at the end of the week the nurse looked and said "OK, Rita, you don't want hospice. I see you are trying to save your child." I said "Yes, I am." We baptized Jacob. It was my kids, Amy and James, and the hospice nurse. I felt as though Jacob was getting sick.

ALL MY CHILDREN

James was having problems in school, and I didn't know what was going on. We attended therapy with James. James had 30 min, and I had 30 min to discuss what they had discussed during his. In the meanwhile, Jacob was in day care. So this took place after school. Later on we found out none of this was changing. The different foods and the drinking of coffee sometimes reverses with a child that has ADD. None of these things were working. I found it difficult to take care of Jacob while trying to find out what was going on with James. Because he was having accidents, he was fighting, couldn't be still, got put in time out, etcetera. So we attended group therapy. This included three other

> Ventilators, also called respirators, are machines that help people breathe when they are unable to breathe on their own. Ventilators pump air into the lungs at a rate and volume adjusted for each individual. If an individual will be on a ventilator for an extended period, a surgeon might create an opening into the windpipe for the insertion of a tracheotomy tube to which the ventilator equipment attaches.

child along with their parents, and this still didn't work. After all the sessions, the therapist wanted to change again. I could not attend the hours that she wanted us to come. At this time, I was on family leave without pay, and Jacob was hospitalized in ICU for a feeding tube. But he had other complications. So we no longer continued therapy with them. So I spoke with someone at another mental health clinic and they visited me. I called their emergency hot line number and someone came within the week. They suggest for me to sign James into their clinic.

In the meanwhile, Jacob was still having problems and they wanted me to take him off of the ventilator. Jacob stayed in the hospital for so long that I had to cut his hair on many occasions. The nursing staff there had knew us so well that they knew my family when they seen them. They start talking about putting a trach in Jacob. They just couldn't get him to come off the vent.

It was so funny, I had a social worker for the HMO and for the hospital. The HMO has their own social worker. I had a visit from these two. I started crying and they said we didn't mean to upset you, we just wanted to help. And then I slash out "Where were you 2 years ago when I need you! The lady that had came to visit after I had Jacob never came back or called to see if I was all right."

After I had Jacob, there was this one group of mothers, Baby Steps, that helped me get signed on with parent–infant training. Which was good, too. They came to the day care for physical therapy.

In the meanwhile, Amy was acting different. She got sick while Jacob was in the hospital. And James, my 8-year-old, was acting out. He got so bad he start saying that I didn't care about him that I only care about Jacob 'cause we were going out there twice a day. I told him that I love him and Amy, and if they were sick it would be the same. He was having so much trouble at school that they wanted to put him in this school where they had highly aggressive kids. I said no, that's not for him. So the mental health center had this school which was really good. He was later diagnosed with having ADD. He would be place in this small group, not in a classroom of 20 to 30 kids in a class. This one was 8 or less. What was good was that they all had the same problem. There was one girl and four or five boys. They had a teacher and helper and therapist. I was finally glad to see that someone else was going through the same thing!

Jacob was still in the hospital. Then my job had decide that I couldn't be on family leave any longer, that I had to come back. I told them that I needed more time because the reason I had taken the time off from work was because of the seizures that Jacob would have in the summertime. One summer he had 15 seizures at one time on the way to the doctor's office.

> The Family and Medical Leave Act was signed into law by President Clinton in 1993. This act provides for mothers and fathers to take up to 12 weeks of unpaid leave for the birth or adoption of a child or to care for an immediate family member with a serious health condition (U.S. Department of Labor, 2001).

OFF THE VENT

I've taken real good care of Jacob so far. I met a lot of families there at the hospital. I couldn't believe how it seemed that the hospital didn't know about Jacob's problem. I told them that Jacob had to have one-on-one nursing. One morning I dropped the kids off at school and I head for the hospital. I would stay until 2:15 p.m., and pick up James and then go to get Amy. So one day I didn't go to the hospital, so I call. I had to rush back because Jacob was doing good after they put his trach in and he was off the vent. They did something I asked them not to. They wanted to move him to another room but he was still too ill. In the meanwhile, the nurse had to watch him and another patient. They called to tell me that his trach fell out. And I had already mentioned that Jacob needed a one-on-one nurse. They had to reenter the trach. We moved to another room after he got better and it was almost time for him to leave the hospital. But before it was time to leave, they had me to spend a night to learn how to use the equipment. They had arranged for a respiratory therapist to come in and show me how to break down the machines. And if there was a problem she showed me what to do.

Before I left I had a talk with the doctor and a traveling nurse whom she and I became very good friends. They took me in a private room and asked me if I wanted to keep Jacob on a vent. They continued to speak of how I should have let Jacob die because of the many expenses. But I asked for them to help me to receive equipment. They started me out with 24-hr nursing and then they dropped the hours from 24 to 16 hr. They sent the message and a certified letter and I was angry. James and Jacob shared a room. I had equipment like a ventilator, battery, oximeter, humidifier, suction machine, oxygen, and a list of other things.

The nurses that came were really nice. Then they started visiting nursing companies. I had one really bad nurse that left in the middle of Jacob's care. She was trying to show me where to set the high and low button. She didn't call the company or anything—she just left and we were stuck because I had to find another nurse in the middle of the night and I had to take the kids to school the next morning. Somehow they found someone to take her place. It was a difficult experience learning about the machine and how to change the trach and soon my children learned how also.

THEY JUST CAN'T ACCEPT IT

The child protective services system (CPS) is widely viewed as a system that is overwhelmed and in crisis. According to the U.S. Department of Health and Human Services (2000), of the 2,806,000 referrals in 1998, approximately two thirds of the referrals warranted investigation. Less than one fifth of all referrals ultimately resulted in a "substantiated" finding of maltreatment.

One day I had a terrible experience! A lady came to my house unexpectedly from CPS. She said someone had called and said I was taking Jacob out without his ventilator and oxygen. But I explained to her that I keep oxygen in my car at all times, and I also had two tanks in my house. She asked me questions, and I explained to the nurse why she was there. The nurse laughed just as I did. She thought it was joke, because she knew that Jacob's vent was not a portable. The caseworker also spoke to a friend of mine to verify who lived in my house and what kind of person I was. I was upset to think how someone could suggest that I was trying to harm Jacob. When all I wanted to do was take care of my baby. She also told me that she knew of more babies that were in a state home east of here. Some days I think maybe I will see about taking in some of those babies. I don't like to think of nobody loving them.

Later on I found out that it was the HMO that called her. They were tired of paying for the nursing care, and even though Jacob had SSI, they still had to pay over $2,000 dollars worth of equipment. The lady would have to investigate another incident that came up. My lights were cut off, and my nurse asked the light company not to turn off the lights. They did it anyway. A call was made to Jacob's doctor about the lights. The lady from CPS received a call from the doctor. I later explained to her I didn't get them in time to pay the bill. I explained to her what happened. She told me I had a good idea who made the call about the lights—it was the HMO again.

Jacob is now much better, but we still have problems with the HMO. I just don't understand how come they can't accept that I love my baby and I want to keep him no matter what the circumstances are. I love all of my children.

Activities

1. According to Dunst, Trivette, and Deal (1994), family centered practices require changes in the conceptualization and implementation of services to those that

(a) are responsive to family concerns and desires, (b) build upon and strengthen child and family capabilities, (c) utilize informal and formal community resources and supports, and (d) create opportunities for children and families to learn skills and acquire competencies that have empowering consequences. Provide evidence in a bulleted list that Rita's service providers were family centered or were not family centered. What further actions could have been more family centered?

2. Review your own health insurance policy and answer the following questions:

   • Does the policy cover hospice services?

   • Does the policy cover home health nurses? What is the maximum number of days covered? Does the insurance company arrange for the nursing care, or do you contract with a company of your choice?

   • What durable medical equipment is covered?

   • How many days of hospital stay are allowed for a mother after the birth of a child who is disabled or ill?

3. *Discuss:* Assume that you are an instructor or facilitator for the Baby Steps program that Rita mentions. Your program has an informational component to provide parents with the information and support that they need to be the most effective parents. How you would go about designing a series of meetings that would best meet Rita's needs?

4. Assume that there is a recognized need for one of the Baby Steps meetings to address how to talk to brothers and sisters about having a sibling with special needs. Design a session to address this issue.

5. Research the day care centers in your area to determine whether any of the centers will accept babies who are medically fragile.

6. Research how you would apply for financial assistance to take care of your family if you could no longer work. What resources are available and what is the application process?

7. Educators must be sensitive to the needs of families with a wide range of reading and writing skills. Determine the readability level of your local school's statement of parental rights.

8. Many hospitals that serve children have an educational program or employ a school liaison. Determine whether your local hospitals offer such programs and invite a representative to speak to your class. Submit a list of the questions that you will ask the speaker, and include questions that will provide answers about the special education services offered and the ways in which they collaborate with parents.

9. Visit a family or a classroom where a child uses a ventilator or has a tracheotomy tube. Ask them to show you what is involved in changing, cleaning, or suctioning.

10. When a person is sent home on a ventilator, family members must learn how to check the equipment and care for the tracheotomy to keep it clean and to prevent problems, such as a clogged tube or an infection. Increasingly, teachers are expected to perform similar procedures as "related services," with training and under the supervision of a

school nurse, public health nurse, or licensed physician. Discuss your level of comfort with performing such related services as tracheotomy suctioning, clean intermittent catheterization, tube feeding, ventilator monitoring, and oxygen administration. What level of training would prepare you to perform these tasks? What knowledge do you have of the court decisions (i.e., *Irving Independent School District v. Tatro*) that require school personnel to provide health services as related services?

11. Rita mentions how glad she was to know that other parents were going through the same thing. Conduct research to locate support groups in your community for parents or siblings of children with disabilities. Call various disability organizations and locate at least three parent or sibling support groups that meet regularly. Develop a list that includes the group name, the name and telephone number of a contact person, the frequency and location of their meetings, and a brief description of what occurs at the meetings.

12. Imagine that you are Rita. Using her voice, create a list of the problems you have encountered. In addition, be prepared to discuss Rita's values and the experiences or beliefs that are influential in the way she approaches problems.

13. *Discuss:* Teachers are sometimes involved in sharing the initial diagnosis with parents. How do educators know how much information to give parents at one time, and how can they support parents after they receive a diagnosis? What support role did Rita's friend play?

14. Rita said that her son received SSI, which stands for Supplemental Security Income. Go to the Social Security Web site, as well as to other Internet sites, and research the eligibility requirements and the benefits of the SSI program.

15. Interview the parent of a child with severe disabilities to learn about their experiences in obtaining support and assistance from private and governmental agencies and organizations.

16. Describe the best practices that teachers and other helping professionals should use to assist this family.

17. Write an analysis of this case, drawing parallels from this case to (a) your own experiences; (b) theory and research from class discussions, course readings, and knowledge gained in previous classes; and (c) other cases in this book.

Suggested Resources

Gandy, A. (1994). Anencephaly. *Pediatric Database (PEDBASE)*. Available for download at www.icondata.com/health/pedbase

Powell, T., & Gallagher, P. (1993). *Brothers and sisters: A special part of exceptional families*. Baltimore: Paul H. Brookes.

Rozycki, A. (1996). Related services under the Individuals With Disabilities Education Act: Health care services for students with complex health care needs [Electronic version]. *BYU Education & Law Journal,* 1996, pp. 67-81. Available for download at www.law2.byu.edu/jel

Online Resources

Visit the Web site at www.voice-center.com/trach_index.html for information on tracheotomy tubes.

In addition, visit the Web site at www.eparent.com/resources/directories/p2p.html for a directory of Parent To Parent programs.

References

Blaska, J. K. (1998). *Cyclical grieving: Reoccurring emotions experienced by parents who have children with disabilities.* (ERIC Document Reproduction Service No. ED419349)

Dunst, C. J., Trivette C. M., & Deal, A. G. (1994). Final thoughts concerning adoption of family-centered intervention practices. In C. J. Dunst, C. M. Trivette, & A. G. Deal (Eds.), *Supporting and strengthening families: Methods, strategies and practices* (pp. 222–225). Cambridge, MA: Brookline Books.

Holland Sentinel. (1999, June 10). *New mothers getting longer hospital stays.* Retrieved June 3, 2001, from www.hollandsentinel.com/stories

Irving Independent School District v. Tatro, 468 U.S. 883 (1984)

National Hospice Foundation. (2002, August). Do-not-resuscitate orders and hospice care. Retrieved February 20, 2004, from www.nhpco.org/i4a/pages/index.cfm?pageid=3563

Schaefer, R. A. (1995). *LLUMC legacy: Daring to care.* Loma Linda, CA: Loma Linda University Medical Center. Retrieved May, 3, 2003, from www.llu.edu

U.S. Department of Health and Human Services, Administration on Children, Youth, and Families. (2000). *Child maltreatment 1998: Reports from the states to the national child abuse and neglect data system.* Washington, DC: U.S. Government Printing Office. Retrieved from www.acf.hhs.gov March 16, 2004 from www. acf.dhhs.gov/programs/cb/publications/cm98/cpt3.htm

U.S. Department of Labor. (2001). *Employment Standards Administration Wage and Hour Division, Fact Sheet, 28: The Family and Medical Leave Act of 1993.* Retrieved May 16, 2001, from www.dol.gov/dol/esa